Stephen Eric Bronner

YO-BZK-744

Rosa Luxemburg
A Revolutionary for Our Times

Columbia University Press
New York

Columbia University Press   Morningside Edition   1987
Columbia University Press   New York

Library of Congress Cataloging-in-Publication Data

Bronner, Stephen Eric, 1949–
    Rosa Luxemburg—a revolutionary for our times. 1981.
    Includes bibliographical references and index.
    1. Luxemburg, Rosa, 1871–1919.   2. Socialists—Germany
—Biography.   3. Revolutionists—Germany—Biography.
I. Bronner, Stephen Eric, 1949–   A revolutionary
for our times,   II. Title.
HX274.7.L89B76   1987   335.4′092′4 [B]   86-31012
ISBN 0-231-06512-4
ISBN 0-231-06513-2 (pbk.)

Columbia University Press
New York   Guildford, Surrey

Printed in the United States of America

This book is Symyth-sewn.

Contents

Acknowledgments

There are a number of people I would like to thank for their support and advice including Stanley Aronowitz, Douglas Kellner, John and Terry Lanigan, and Richard Wolff. Also I would like to express my gratitude to Peter Ayrton and Richard Kuper of Pluto for their help with the manuscript. In particular, however, I want to express my deepest thanks to Rosalyn Baxandall and Joel Rogers for their intellectual insight, their encouragement, and their friendship.

In memory of Henry M. Pachter   1907–1980

Preface to the Morningside Edition

Viewed politically, the years since the original publication of this volume in 1981 have been quite grim. Progressive regimes in the Third World have come under siege. The East has shut the door on insurgent movements for workers' democracy like Solidarity. In the West, a tide of reaction has led to the victory of Reagan in America, Mulroney in Canada, Thatcher in England, Chirac in France, and Kohl in Germany.

Against this backdrop, the struggle continues over Rosa Luxemburg's memory. In this respect, the growth of new "social movements" has played a significant role. While socialist or class forms of identification have declined, these movements have fostered a new commitment to ethnic, national, and sexual modes of self-identification. As a Jew, a Pole, and a woman, Rosa Luxemburg's dramatic life has thus become open to appropriation from various perspectives.

Sometimes this had led to distortions, especially when more attention is given to *what she was* than to *what she believed*. Certain exhibitions dealing with the Jewish heritage in twentieth-century Europe, for example, have occasionally chosen to simply treat Rosa Luxemburg as one of their own. Fanatically anti-Communist Polish nationalists often mention her name alongside that of her life-long enemy, the fascist dictator Marshal Josef Pilsudski. Then too, in a far more sophisticated way, the noted scholar and activist Raya Dunayevskaya recently stressed her contribution to the Women's Liberation Movement, while the important German director, Margarethe von Trotta, just finished a film about Rosa Luxemburg that places first emphasis on her feminism.

At first blush, such efforts seem unobjectionable and may even prove politically useful. Rosa Luxemburg fought tenaciously for her personal independence, and for that of the women in her circle as well. She confronted the sexism of many socialist com-

1

rades in the Second International. She showed that a woman could become a major theorist, a superb orator, and a leading revolutionary activist. She was intellectually rigorous and honest – almost to a fault. Indeed, Rosa Luxemburg is clearly a wonderful symbol for feminists and a superb role model for young people whose first exposure to politics might well come through existing "social movements."

Still, Rosa Luxemburg always opposed the attempt to "transform political questions into personal, sentimental ones." She never defined herself either as a "Jew," a "Pole," or a "woman." She consistently opposed Polish nationalism and had little use for the Jewish Bund, which was so influential in her time. In the same vein, she disagreed with Lili Braun (who desired a separate women's movement) and all those who wanted to organize without primary regard for a class standpoint. Though Rosa Luxemburg was an exemplary woman, the truth is that she never made a major contribution to either a uniquely feminist theory or a particularly feminist practice. Indeed, she always saw herself as an international socialist whose primary loyalty and self-identification derived from her commitment to the abolition of capitalism and the struggle for socialist democracy.

Both social democratic reformists and communist authoritarians, however, have had their difficulties in dealing with Rosa Luxemburg's legacy. The reasons quite obviously involve her politics. Ironically, however, even further explorations into her personal life have drawn attention to this matter, like the recent discovery of certain letters which confirm that her last lover was the political maverick, Paul Levi.

Levi was a committed socialist and Luxemburg's lawyer during the last years of her imprisonment as an opponent of World War I. They were obviously close, and it was to cure Levi's somewhat uncritical admiration for the Bolsheviks that Luxemburg initially wrote her prophetic pamphlet, *The Russian Revolution*. But, fearing that its criticisms of the new workers state might ideologically aid the counterrevolution, she accepted Levi's entreaties not to publish the piece. It was shortly before Rosa Luxemburg's death during the Spartacus revolt of 1919 that she entrusted the work to his keeping.

Soon enough, Paul Levi became the leader of the German

2

Communist Party (KPD) which had emerged from the old Spartacus League. He became known for championing democracy within the movement, criticizing bureaucratic dogmatism, attempting to build the self-administrative capacities of the working class, linking reform and revolution, and opposing Soviet attempts to dominate the new Communist International. All of these commitments, of course, were continuous with Luxemburg's own and quickly created problems for Paul Levi with the Comintern leadership.

The Russian Revolution and the close of World War 1 had raised radical expectations. Recognition that the fledgling workers' state desperately needed foreign support mixed with a throughly romantic revolutionary zeal. Thus, in 1920, many important leaders of the Communist International, like the Hungarian Bela Kun, were demanding an "offensive strategy" that would everywhere call for an immediate seizure of power.

Paul Levi felt that these Comintern leaders were blind to the actual conditions in which a decimated European working class found itself following the failure of the Spartacus revolt and other such ventures. In accord with the spirit of Rosa Luxemburg's thought, he opposed those who wished to make revolution by decree. Instead, Paul Levi sought to turn the KPD into a mass organization by working with trade unions, running candidates for parliament, and fashioning reforms, while still ideologically preparing workers for future revolutionary action.

Debate raged throughout the Communist International. Finally, Lenin and Trotsky came down on the side of Bela Kun. A revolt was planned and, in 1921, the German "March Action" took place, which was quickly and brutally crushed. Levi was furious and publicly demanded that the leadership of the Communist International assume responsibility for the defeat. Though Paul Levi's own political standpoint could easily have served as the basis for Lenin's pamphlet, *Left-Wing Communism: An Infantile Disorder,* the Soviet leader saw the German's criticisms as a breach of discipline and expelled him from the organization.

It was in the aftermath of the March Action that Paul Levi gave Rosa Luxemburg's pamphlet a title and published it. *The Russian Revolution* appeared in 1922 amid tremendous uproar. The fact that the work was published by a "traitor" along with

3

the sharp attacks on Bolshevik authoritarianism, which expressed the feelings of many within the Communist International, caused a sensation. It was not very long before Ruth Fischer, a protege of Zinoviev who would centralize and "bolshevize" the KPD even more once she took power, began demanding a cure for the "syphilitic Luxemburg bacillus" which had infected the party.

But the story is not quite over. Paul Levi was also similar to Rosa Luxemburg in his dislike of sectarianism. Following his expulsion from the Communist movement, he therefore decided to join the German Social Democratic Party (SPD). Unfortunately, if Paul Levi was too democratic and honest for the Communists, his commitment to a radical transformation of capitalism was too strong for the Social Democrats. Isolated within the SPD, ostracized and smeared by the Communists, in despair over Germany's political future, Paul Levi committed suicide in 1930.

It is through stories such as this that the values which underpin Rosa Luxemburg's political heritage become evident. Though the strains of an old orthodoxy still appear in her work, Rosa Luxemburg's thought advances an ethics of political responsibility and honesty. Her conception of socialist democracy was fundamentally predicated on the integrity of the individual along with a sense of reciprocity and trust. Indeed, she clearly understood that the power of capital ultimately rests on the political divisions that exist among working people.

Using a modern vocabulary, Rosa Luxemburg was concerned with "equality" rather than "difference." Organizationally, she therefore saw social democracy as a movement that would respond to "all the oppressed victims of bourgeois society." That unity was to arise from the standpoint of goals which were *universal* in their socialist implications: the constriction of arbitrary socioeconomic and political power along with the empowerment of working people through the development of popular democratic institutions.

The lives of Rosa Luxemburg, and many of her followers like Paul Levi, show how difficult it is to maintain a commitment to such goals. Still, it is precisely in the periods of retreat that they must be kept alive. Amid the calls for "realism," "retrenchment," "austerity," and "compromise," Rosa Luxemburg's radical political theory sharpens the contradictions while the drama

4

of her life strengthens the spirit of resistance. But, ultimately, any judgment of her relevance depends upon a judgment regarding the relevance of those values and goals for which she stood. That she forces each generation to confront them is truly what continues to make Rosa Luxemburg a "revolutionary for our times."

Preface

There are few monuments to the socialist pursuit of freedom, but the life of Rosa Luxemburg is surely one of them. Her personal bravery as well as her work will always serve as an affront to both political vacillation and authoritarianism. Indeed, this remarkable woman stands at the forefront of an emancipatory heritage within marxism which opposes the prevailing deformations of socialism in both the west and the east.

Based upon an accommodation with capitalist exploitation, western social democracy presents a complacent image of managerial responsibility in its acceptance of both bourgeois democracy and reform through compromise. On the other hand, the eastern bloc presents a grey image of socialism – a socialism of dictatorship and concrete, of repression, censorship, queues and party dogmatism. If these two forms were the sum potential of marxism, then there would be no reason to work for the systematic abolition of capitalism.

From Rosa Luxemburg's thought, however, a marxist project emerges which strains against the shackles of both capitalist and socialist oppression. In both her politics and her theory, her perspective was neither dogmatic, opportunist, nor bureaucratic. She does not dote on some 'objectivistic' historical determinism nor on the supposed infallibility of the party in determining the road to freedom. Instead, her thought calls for working people to take control of their own collective destiny without sacrificing the claims of the individual to party decrees.

Centred in a profound understanding of praxis, Luxemburg's thought never surrenders theory to expedient calls for activism or anti-intellectualism. Democracy in everyday life, respect for individual rights, workers' control over the production and distribution of wealth, willingness to experiment and solidarity; these are the basis tenets of a vision which realises

7

the intrinsic connection between socialism and democracy.

Following her death, Luxemburg's thought was shunted to the margin of a political practice dominated by reformism and Stalinism. The force of her vision was, however, never completely extinguished. Indeed, Rosa Luxemburg's work is the legacy of a dedicated socialist whose influence extended from the revolts that shook Europe in 1918-23 to the student revolts of the late sixties. Furthermore, she has helped give birth to a tradition that stands outside the mainstream of 'orthodox' marxism. The impact of Luxemburg's thought has been felt from Korsch and Lukacs to Dutschke and Bahro, from the Workers' Opposition in Russia to the Dutch council communists.

At stake is the socialist project of emancipation, a project which has shown itself once again in the country of her birth. Continuing a tradition that has roots in the last century, the Polish working class has again flexed its muscles through a mass strike – a concept which is fundamental to Luxemburg's thought – in order to elaborate the democratic moment that lies at the heart of socialism.

It is possible to question the *subjective* motives of various individuals in the Polish working class. But the real issue involves the manner in which the demands of this class are *objectively* socialist in character. These major demands speak for themselves: the right to strike, abolition of censorship, free trade unions, respect for the conventions of the International Labour Organisation, abolition of commercial and economic privileges for party officials, public discussion of and participation in production goals, as well as the democratisation of the party itself.

All these demands conform to Luxemburg's conception of socialism. But no movement can simply be equated with the particular demands which it puts forward. There is a spirit in a movement, and it is this which makes Luxemburg a contemporary of the events in Poland in 1980 and 1981.

As against certain traditional and current notions of orthodoxy, Luxemburg never believed that the interests of the Party were identical with the interests of the working class. It was Luxemburg who most clearly articulated the socialist necessity for 'self-administration' (*Selbsttätigkeit*) by the working class – a notion which lies at the very core of the current struggle – and she

8

always believed that it was more important for the working class to make mistakes and learn from them than for a central committee to implement the 'correct line'. For she saw that capacities for self-administration would develop only through the dialectical tension between party and mass, organisation and spontaneity.

Of course, due to the tactical inability to oppose the ruling Party with another 'party', Luxemburg's specific prescription does not apply – though now a link between *Solidarity* and significant elements in the Party has occurred. But, obviously, *Solidarity* was never simply concerned with 'economism' or beset by 'trade union consciousness'. By unifying the disparate sectors of the working class, and seeking to translate economic demands into political ones. *Solidarity* has shown a real affinity with Luxemburg's thought.

A new path is being forged by the Polish workers. No matter what the future holds for the specific concessions that have been extracted from the regime, two sweeping admissions have been made that cannot be withdrawn. By granting that the Polish workers have the right to free trade unions and open elections, 'actually existing socialism' (Bahro) has openly admitted that its political organ (the Party) does not have the exclusive privilege of controlling all aspects of social and political life. By allowing opposing views into the official media, the choice of delegates to a Party Congress by secret ballot and the running of factories in a non-authoritarian manner, the Party has been forced to concede the importance of democracy to a working class that is not identical with those rulers who claim to speak in its name.

But most importantly, as Rosa Luxemburg already foresaw, it has come to be publicly admitted that socialism is not some finished political product whose realisation is defined by bureaucratically nationalising the means of production, undemocratically developing a centralised plan, or having an authoritarian Communist Party in power. Rather, socialism has at last come to be seen as a process which seeks to extend the transformation of political and economic relations in terms of ever greater democratic control over society by the workers themselves.

9

Of course, nationalism and religion have played a role in these events in Poland, and Rosa Luxemburg was an arch-enemy of both. But it must be understood that 'proletarian internationalism' is currently nothing other than a slogan which seeks to hide the interests of the Soviet nation-state. Given previous attempts to export revolution 'on bayonets' and the pervasive fear brought about by various exercises of Soviet domination, Polish nationalism is inextricably linked to the fear of invasion. Yet, there is also an internationalist potential in the events themselves. The rage of Party bureaucrats throughout the eastern bloc attests to the possibility that the democratic demands of the Polish workers will serve as a symbol that will spread to other nations under Soviet domination.

It is true that Poland is overwhelmingly Catholic. The repressive policies of the Party apparatus have done little to undermine the influence of the Church, although belief that the Pope's visit, or the real courage shown by many members of the Church, is the prime cause of recent events is simply foolish. In the same way as Rosa Luxemburg analysed the development of the mass strike, recent events in Poland must be seen in terms of a *process* of strike actions – from 1956 to 1970 to 1980 – that have grown ever more politically mature in the type of demands that have been put forward. Whenever the Church tried to exert a 'moderating influence' on the workers over the past few months the workers would not listen. Surely, a measure of criticism can be raised. But, to the same degree that it is impossible to make a revolution by fiat, so it is impossible to erase religion by decree. If the force of religion is to be surmounted, then – as Marx fully understood – the actual conditions of existence which make religion a need for so many must themselves be overcome.

By now it should be clear to anyone that the actions of the Polish workers have not been directed to the creation of some capitalist-nationalist-theocracy, but rather to the extension of democracy and socialism. Though bourgeois politicians may well have sought to exploit the events for their own purposes, responsible journalists – such as Flora Lewis and John Darnton of *The New York Times*, as well as I. F. Stone who emphasised the affinity between the Polish workers' demands and Luxemburg's concerns – have been forced to conclude that the Polish working

10

class is fighting for more socialism and not less.

What would more socialism involve? Nothing other than that the working class itself share in the formulation of socio-economic policy, express its unrecognised demands in political terms, and begin to build its own public culture.

Such concerns are fundamental to Rosa Luxemburg's vision of socialism which seeks the *extension* of democracy through the socialisation of the means of production – to deepen the workers' own capacities for self-administration. Thus the democratisation of society as a whole becomes the goal of socialism – a goal which is anything but static or finished and which has its own tradition within marxism.

In view of the repression that has been justified in the name of socialism, the recovery of this emancipatory tradition within marxism has become ever more crucial. For there can be little doubt that many people still continue to picture the socialist society in terms of a Marx-Lenin-Stalin lineage. Rosa Luxemburg helps to articulate an alternative. From her work, it is possible to learn how the construction of socialism demands that the imagination burst the bonds of cynicism, false pragmatism and authoritarianism. Whether it be in her theoretical analysis of the mass strike or her criticisms of the Russian Revolution, her description of a war weary nation or her reflections on literature from a prison cell: for Rosa Luxemburg, the world, like the self, is open, capable of change, and in constant need of being changed.

When she writes that 'I, too, am a land of boundless possibilities,' the thought of a new socialism – a socialism of colour and life – begins to emerge. This is the thought that the tradition in which she plays such an essential role seeks to actualise.

1. Childhood and Youth

Rosa Luxemburg was born in the small Polish city of Zamosc in 1871, the year of the Paris Commune. Her family exemplified the cosmopolitan attitudes of 'enlightened' Jewry; they had no ties to the strong and cultured Jewish community of the town and in 1873 her father, a timber merchant, moved them to Warsaw. Amid her family's fluctuating financial circumstances, Rosa Luxemburg grew up in Poland as a Jew who spoke German at home. It was in her family circle that she learned of Schiller and the Enlightenment with its international ideals. She was to retain many of these attitudes in later life; the famous Jewish socialist organisation – the *Bund* – held no attraction and her concerns always transcended nationality.[1]

It could hardly be said that she remained on intimate terms with her family, although it is possible to discern a bond in her letters. When, for instance, the father of her friend, Hans Diefenbach, fell ill, she advised Hans to return home. Indeed, Luxemburg wrote to Diefenbach – the man closest to her towards the end of her life – that:

> Later one always blames oneself bitterly for every hour which one took away from the old people. I wasn't lucky enough even to have done as little as that. After all, I constantly had to look after the urgent business of humanity and make the world a happier place. And so I received the news of my father's death in Berlin, where I had been wrangling with Jaurès, Millerand, Daszýnski, Bebel, and God knows who else until the feathers flew. In the meantime, the old gentleman wasn't able to wait any longer. Probably he said to himself that there would be no sense anyway in waiting, however long he waited; after all, I never did 'have time' for him or myself – and he died.

When I came back from Paris, he had already been buried a week. Now, of course, I would be much wiser, but one is usually wiser after it's too late.[2]

Although they did not have much in common politically, her father was able to show a large measure of tolerance when Rosa, still in high school, became involved in radical politics. Indeed, in 1906, he even helped bail her out of a Polish jail.

During these early years, she joined the *Proletariat* party. Founded in 1882 by Ludwik Warynski, *Proletariat* was the first Polish socialist party.[3] Its main opposition on the left was the *Polish People* party which was founded by Boleslaw Limanowski to emphasise the independence of Poland from Russia. In the eyes of the authorities, there were only minor differences between these groups. Yet, though their demands often overlapped and though personality conflicts often proved as crucial as real political differences, the national question – which would wrack Polish socialism long after these original groups had disappeared – divided them from the very start.

What distinguished the *Proletariat* group was its internationalist standpoint. Its organisers sought to bolster class consciousness by putting forward economic demands and opposing 'romantic' ideas such as the national liberation of Poland that would deflect or compromise this consciousness. Though the *Proletariat* did not rule out the use of terror in principle – which sometimes resulted in an uneasy alliance with the famous Russian *Narodnaya Volya* (People's Will), an organisation that was highly centralised and supported individual acts of terror – the tactic was subordinated to the group's basic organisational project: the creation of a mass base.

Throughout her life Luxemburg retained the belief in a mass party as the builder of a revolutionary, internationalist, class consciousness. But, the *Proletariat* itself was decimated after the strike wave of the 1880s; its principal leaders were either hanged or died in prison and the rest of its members were under police surveillance. Unable to organise a mass base and hunted by the police, Rosa Luxemburg fled to Zurich in 1887.

It was there that she began her socialist apprenticeship in earnest; she studied Marx and Engels seriously for the first time

14

and entered into the world of radical emigré life with its endless personal quarrels and intense intellectual friendships.[4] It was also in Zurich that she met her great love and political mentor: Leo Jogiches.[5] Almost alone among the major universities of Europe, the one in Zurich had a 'lenient' policy towards admitting women and Luxemburg studied mathematics, natural science, law, and political economy there.

Rosa Luxemburg was immediately recognised as a brilliant student and her dissertation *The Industrial Development of Poland* was accorded the rare honour of being published as a book. Its arguments served as a theoretical complement of and justification for the political position which she held while still a member of *Proletariat*. It set out to show that Polish industrial development was dependent upon the growth of the Russian market and Russian capitalism. Consequently the Polish proletariat's quest for a nation state would necessarily hinder the development of productive forces in that country. In economic terms, nationalism would be a self-defeating strategy for the Polish working class. But, Luxemburg also saw that support for nationalism would compromise the Polish working class politically. From a nationalist standpoint, the abolition of Tsarism would obviously become a secondary concern and the emphasis upon the uniqueness of the Polish working class would detract from its international responsibilities.[6] More importantly, however, Luxemburg believed that the Polish workers would actually be betraying their own interests by emphasising the creation of a 'class state' which would ultimately serve and support the control of the bourgeoisie.[7]

Luxemburg always sought to derive political consequences for the working class from her economic enquiries. The arguments in her dissertation thus came to serve as the basis for the journal *Sprawa Robotnicza* (The Workers' Voice) which she and Jogiches founded in 1893, the year in which another strike wave that involved sixty thousand workers hit the city of Lodz.

This event proved decisive in the formation of the Polish Socialist Party (PPS), a party that would more and more fall under the direction of the two men who were to become Rosa Luxemburg's arch enemies within the movement for Polish socialism. These were Ignaz Daszyński and Josef Pilsudski who later defected from socialism altogether and – running parallel to Mussolini's political trajectory – became the dictator of Poland in the twenties.

Under the direction of these two figures, the PPS was led into the nationalist camp. Luxemburg's minority faction, which supported Polish national autonomy within a democratic federal Russian Republic, split off in 1895 and merged with the Social Democratic Party of Lithuania in 1900.[8] The result was the Social Democratic Party of the Kingdom of Poland and Lithuania (SDKPL) – a party that stressed the principle of international working class solidarity which Rosa Luxemburg would advocate all her life.

2. Nationalism and Internationalism

Given the influence of Lenin's theory of 'national self-determination'. Stalin's notion of 'socialism in one country', and the popular identification of the left with 'national liberation' movements, it is difficult to remember that internationalism was once a cornerstone of radical socialist thought. With the exception of the mass strike, there is no single idea which has become so associated with Rosa Luxemburg. It is an idea that has stirred enormous controversy and has given rise to many misunderstandings: it also retains an extraordinary relevance for the present.

In the simplest terms, Luxemburg argued that an equal partnership between nationalism and socialism was impossible. Yet, like Marx, she recognised the need for agitation within national boundaries.[1] This was never an issue. Her point was only that national boundaries and national identity could not simply be *accepted* as permanent political and cultural divisions within the proletariat, if the latter was to defeat the bourgeoisie and its ideology. For this reason, Luxemburg believed that socialism must offer a *qualitative* alternative to the nationalism promulgated by a bourgeoisie that had long forsaken its progressive role. She wrote:

> For a workers' party, nationality is a question both of programme and of class organisation. The position that a workers' party assumes on the nationality question, as on every other question, must differ in method and basic approach from the positions of even the most radical bourgeois parties, and from the positions of the pseudo-socialistic, petit bourgeois parties.[2]

Luxemburg was calling for the application of Marxist method to the issue of nationalism. No trans-historical dogma is possible; each situation must be evaluated specificially in terms

17

of a socialist and inevitably internationalist alternative. For Luxemburg, the organisational alternative became a living reality in the form of the Second International. And it was the existence of this organisational alternative, along with her demand for specificity, that led her to criticise Marx's own views on Poland in terms of the marxist method itself.

From her standpoint, Marx and Engels – as well as the leading lights of the Second International – saw the Polish situation solely from the standpoint of German social democracy and the needs of the bourgeois revolution in western Europe. She wrote:

> by failing to analyse Poland and Russia as class societies bearing economic and political contradictions in their bosoms, by viewing them not from the point of view of historical development but as if they were in a fixed, absolute condition as homogeneous, undifferentiated units, this view ran counter to the very essence of marxism.[3]

Given the political thrust of the SDKPL, it is possible to say that Luxemburg failed to comprehend Marx's strategic idea: that the national revolution is an opening to the permanent international revolution. In a certain sense, however, this is beside the point. Whether her economic analysis in *The Industrial Development of Poland* holds or not, Luxemburg used the marxist method to shatter what had become a point of dogma and raised the crucial issue which is relevant for every socialist movement on every issue.

As she put it: 'there is one question that takes precedence over all others for us Polish socialists in adopting a position on any social phenomenon: what are the implications of that position for the class interests of the Polish proletariat?'[4] In regard to nationalism, this implies that any positive evaluation of a national movement would depend on whether its success could potentially guarantee the sovereignty necessary for national autonomy as well as the creation of a political arena that would further the possibilities of building international class consciousness amongst the working class.

It would completely counteract the thrust of Luxemburg's thought to argue that her analysis precludes the possibility of revolutionary activity within national boundaries. Of course, in a new set of conditions, Luxemburg did claim that national wars were no longer possible.[5] Clearly, she was far less prescient than Lenin – and even Stalin – in foreseeing the extraordinary appeal of nationalism to the colonised Third World.

In his famous debate with Rosa Luxemburg over 'the right of self-determination', Lenin argued as follows: precisely because socialism proceeds from an *internationalist* standpoint, it must respect equality among nations and national cultures.[6] For this reason, national oppression of one predominant group over another minority group within a nation cannot be tolerated, especially when the particular culture of that oppressed minority does not receive expression.

The question is whether this position ultimately undermines internationalism itself by justifying bourgeois national movements. Against this charge Lenin suggested that, though every nation has the 'right' to self-determination, this right is not necessarily going to be exercised since the economic development of capitalism is international in scope. Particularly in the case of smaller countries, it would be in the interests of all nations to amalgamate themselves in a larger organisation.[7] Moreover, Lenin argued that only the 'progressive' elements in national movements should be supported; i.e. those elements which do not foster bourgeois ideology and deflect proletarian consciousness.[8] Consequently, from Lenin's standpoint, the working class would only be giving a 'negative' support to bourgeois national movements in their attempts to overcome national oppression since 'beyond that begins the "positive" activity of the *bourgeoisie* striving to *fortify* nationalism'.[9] Lastly, Lenin took great pains to differentiate his position from that of Otto Bauer and the Austro-Marxists who essentially supported 'cultural-national autonomy' within a federated state.[10]

Lenin believed that all languages and cultures must be treated with egalitarian respect from an internationalist standpoint. But any identification on the part of the working class – whether it be national, racial, or ethnic – that would prevent the development of international harmony or an international social democratic culture would have to be avoided. In Lenin's view, however, the primacy of the economic moment would preclude such a development and he could assume that the minorities

19

within a nation-state would learn the dominant language since it would be in their commercial interest to do so.

Despite Lenin's support for Stalin's essay on the national question,[11] Lenin's original perspective largely resists the dogma into which it has since been incorporated. For Lenin's position on the national question – at least until 1920 – rests fundamentally on the twin belief in internationalism and democratic choice as well as upon equality among nations within an international community. The sophistry that lies behind current Soviet pronouncements on 'proletarian internationalism' – which identify internationalism with support for the particular policy choices of the 'fatherland of the revolution' – goes against Lenin's demand for equality.[12] By the same token, the 'Great Russian chauvinism,' the anti-semitism and discrimination which mark the current Soviet regime would have been repugnant to Lenin. From his standpoint, the subjugation of the eastern bloc by the Soviet Union is without real theoretical justification. Though particular examples may be found to dispute the claim, such as Lenin's China policy, his overriding emphasis upon the international revolution cannot be ignored. Indeed, Lenin's foreign policy is a far cry from Stalin's and from the arbitrary support that current Soviet leaders have given to many reactionary nationalist groupings.[13]

Still, there are fundamental problems that derive from the mechanistic nature of Lenin's formulation – problems a Luxemburgian position picks out. Thus, *in the national struggle itself*, Lenin's abstract differentiation between 'negative' and 'positive' support for a bourgeois movement collapses; this 'negative' support turns into its opposite precisely because of the central emphasis upon the oppressor to be overcome. Lenin's assumption that the working class will not *ultimately* be seduced by the ideology of nationalism while fighting for the creation of a nation-state has in practice been shown to be unwarranted.

Of course, under certain circumstances, this purity can be preserved and Lenin gives an important theoretical justification for tactical collaboration with the 'progressive' wing of the bourgeoisie. But, clearly, Lenin's mechanistic assertion that economic interest would necessarily foster internationalism on

20

the part of the working classes of the smaller, less-advanced states did not materialise.

Especially where the working class is weak and lacks its own political organisation and/or revolutionary tradition, the maintenance of class consciousness in opposition to bourgeois nationalism becomes difficult. As Luxemburg correctly observed, precisely to the extent that the working class is fighting with the bourgeoisie for a *class state*, it is fighting against its own ultimate interests.[14]

This becomes apparent in her criticism of the slogan, 'the right of self-determination':

> What is especially striking about this formula is the fact that it doesn't represent anything specifically connected with socialism or with the politics of the working class. (It) is at first glance a paraphrase of the old slogan of bourgeois nationalism put forth in all countries at all times: 'the right of nations to freedom and independence'.[15]

Thus, revolutionary class consciousness is already seduced once it accepts a notion of abstract 'right' that is quintessentially bourgeois in nature; from Luxemburg's standpoint, Lenin accepts a concept of the nation

> which is one of those categories of bourgeois ideology which Marxist theory submitted to a radical revision, showing how that misty veil, like the concepts of the 'freedom of citizens', 'equality before the law', etc., conceals in every case a definite historical content.[16]

Luxemburg realised that nationalism, when advanced by socialists, always retains a reformist component and that reformism is inherently tied to nationalism. Not only does nationalism call for the unification of ultimately divergent interests but also a fundamental interest in preserving the status quo – organisationally as well as ideologically – arises within socialist movements which seek such a unification.[17]

In this regard, Lenin perceived a fundamental contradiction which he ultimately could not resolve: bourgeois society would give rise to national liberation movements at the same time that it fostered the internationalisation of capital. On the other hand

Luxemburg understood that nationalism would deflect the consciousness of the working class and that a new mode of organisation and thinking would be necessary to confront international capital.

Both Lenin and Luxemburg argued their positions in terms of a presupposition which is no longer valid: the existence of a viable socialist international.[18] Lenin's views, especially, become outdated and open to the worst manipulation when there is no supra-national organisation. Here, Luxemburg provides a corrective, perceiving that nationalism is a real force which cannot simply be manipulated by a revolutionary socialist movement. The nation-state and nationalism are strictly historical phenomena which, in a new period, will need to be surmounted by an alternative form of working class organisation and consciousness.

Precisely at the time when a viable international organisation and consciousness are most necessary, nationalism, sectarianism, and separatism have come to dominate large portions of the left. Isolationism, protectionism, provincialism, uncritical 'Third Worldism' and nationalism do not provide the resolution for a contradiction that can no longer be ignored: the objective contradiction between the multinationals and the nation state. This is a basic contradiction which exists over and beyond that between various sectors of capital and the working class within a given national arena.

A 'new international division of labour' is effectively creating the objective conditions for an international working class. But this development within capital which results in business competition for production sites throughout the globe has not been accompanied by a rise in the international consciousness of the working class. The Second and Third Internationals have collapsed – it is time for a new orientation of consciousness based upon an old dream. The new developments within capitalism bode ill for a class whose divisions obscure its need for an order that will abolish exploitation by multinationals and create international standards for work safety, wages, education and all the other basic demands of socialism.

From Luxemburg's standpoint, socialism will either be international or it will not be at all. Her critique of nationalism

22

retains its relevance precisely to the extent that it calls for a new perspective in confronting the most essential issues of the contemporary world from a socialist stance.

In her own time, Rosa Luxemburg embodied her view in the slogan that 'the International is the fatherland of the proletariat'. It was no accident that she should be led to the country whose socialist party was the most advanced in theory and, supposedly, closest to revolution: the German Social Democratic Party (SPD). When Rosa had finished her thesis and been introduced to German socialist circles in Zurich, the expert on Polish socialism entered a marriage of convenience with a German citizen, Gustav Lubeck. This marriage enabled her to emigrate to Berlin, the city in which she would make her name in the SPD and also the city in which she would be brutally murdered in a workers' revolt that was opposed by the very same party which she had initially held in such high esteem.

3. A Revolutionary in the West: The Party in Context

When Rosa Luxemburg entered the German social democratic world in 1898, Karl Marx had already been dead for fifteen years and the working class movement had entered a new phase of political development.[1] The revolutions of 1848 had failed, the Paris Commune had been crushed, and the First International lay in ruins. The Second International had arisen from the ashes and the SPD stood at its forefront

Formed in 1875, the SPD was the first of the modern social democratic parties and also the strongest. Given its vigour and tenacity – reflected in its extraordinary growth and electoral success[2] – it is no wonder that other parties should have looked to the German socialists for leadership and that the Austrians, Belgians and Swiss, amongst others, should have followed the German organisational model.

The Party itself was created at Gotha by the merger of the two leading German working class organisations. The first, the *Allgemeiner Deutscher Arbeiterverein*, was inspired by its founder, Ferdinand Lassalle who advocated state co-operatives and reformist political activity within the existing state structure. This organisation had opposed the second, more marxist, group, commonly known as the *Eisenachers*, who were in principle far more concerned with the seizure of state power and the proletarian expropriation of the means of production. The dual heritage of Marx and Lassalle was to influence the entire development of German socialism even to the extent that the differences in their outlooks came to be reflected in the factions that formed within the SPD.

Yet, from the moment of its emergence, the SPD was a force to be reckoned with. As a consequence of the enormous increase in capital accumulation, industrialisation, and urbanisation in the latter part of the nineteenth century – including the

24

years of depression that began in 1873 – the proletariat, as well as the 'industrial reserve army', grew rapidly.[3] Correspondingly, a growth in the class consciousness of this proletariat took place; anti-imperialist, distrustful of the nationalist sloganeering of the Kaiser, and aware of its material oppression, the proletariat was truly a 'state within a state'. That isolation was enhanced by the practical activity of the SPD which, like the other social democratic organisations of Europe, principally directed its efforts to industrial workers. This was what allowed the SPD to be a mass party from its very inception. But, as a 'mass party', it had to accommodate conflicting tendencies and opinions and this made theory, ideology and access to the press essential topics to people with views as different as those of Eduard Bernstein and Rosa Luxemburg.

Newspapers like the *Sächsiche Arbeiter Zeitung* (on the SPD left) and *Sozialistische Monatshefte* (on the SPD right) quickly gained their followings. But the prestige of *Die Neue Zeit*, a private paper which was generally regarded as the party's official organ, was never rivalled. Its editor, Karl Kautsky, was the acknowledged 'pope' of marxism and passed for Marx and Engels' philosophical heir.[4]

Whatever the later criticisms of his philosophical interpretations of marxism,[5] Kautsky bequeathed to the movement a theoretical consistency that was fundamental to its development. This became particularly evident when, in collaboration with Bernstein, he was entrusted with writing the now classic *Erfurt Programme* which synthesised the views of the SPD. But perhaps synthesis is not quite the right word for what Kautsky achieved: the *Erfurt Programme* of 1890 was divided into a radical theoretical section that emphasised revolutionary change and a section of immediate demands that were essentially reformist in nature. In contrast to *The Communist Manifesto*, the specific demands were never linked to the overriding goal to be achieved. A dichotomy resulted between the subjective sense of a revolutionary socialist purpose and the reformism that would be objectively carried on in day-to-day practice, which would later come to haunt the movement during the 'revisionism debate'. In a sense the division in the *Erfurt Programme* also gave the seal of approval to the conflict between reformists and 'revolu-

25

tionaries' as it opened a space within the Party for what would later emerge as the 'centre'.

Holding together such an uneasy alliance of opinions and factions was no easy task. Charged with this mission were the two men who, with Kautsky, served as Rosa Luxemburg's patrons in the Party: August Bebel[6] and Wilhelm Liebknecht. Both had known Marx and Engels, and both had already paid a price for their socialist convictions long before Rosa Luxemburg's arrival in Germany.

As members of the Reichstag, both had been imprisoned for treason when they opposed the Franco-Prussian war and the German annexation of Alsace-Lorraine. Where Bebel had gained great fame for his oratory, journalism and political acumen, Liebknecht – whose son Karl was to become Rosa Luxemburg's comrade in martyrdom – was far less flamboyant and was known primarily for his organisational skills. Where the one was positively revered by the masses, the other was accorded an overflowing respect. But, in fact, like so many of their comrades both men mirrored the contradiction that stemmed from the situation in which social democracy found itself: they were, at one and the same time, revolutionaries and bureaucratic reformists.

The political position of the SPD was precarious from the beginning. Fearful of the SPD's growing influence amongst the working class, and the political power it could wield, Bismarck implemented the Anti-Socialist laws. From 1878 to 1890 the SPD could not legally organise. Repression against socialists was legally justified; they were effectively excluded from the state. This legislation imposed tremendous pressure and heavy costs upon the SPD which amounted to a trauma that manifested itself in an obsession with legality from which the party would never fully recover.

During the period of the Anti-Socialist laws, '332 labour organisations were dissolved, 1,300 newspapers and periodicals suppressed, about nine hundred party activists driven from their homes and fifteen hundred sentenced to a total of a thousand years in prison'.[7] Then, there was social ostracism, and general paranoia to be contended with. Confronting this Anti-Socialist legislation demanded all the courage, vigour and tenacity that party could muster. In conjunction with the changing socio-economic conditions and the rigid class structure of society, the SPD's opposition to political oppression created a fierce loyalty to the party on the part of the masses. Yet, the very qualities which made for the success of the party stood in marked contrast to the complacency that set in once this success had been achieved.

The Anti-Socialist laws relegated the entire SPD to an underground and oppositionalist existence that led it – as a 'mass party' – to seek legality, emphasise universal suffrage, and concentrate on trade union legislation. These concerns, and the party's later course, were also influenced by the fact that the call for democracy – a revolutionary demand insofar as it projected the creation of a different state to the one over which the Kaiser presided – had passed into the hands of the working class. It was not simply a matter of choice either, since this demand had been abandoned by the bourgeoisie after the failed revolution of 1848. Indeed, the basic issues of the major internal party debates – in which Rosa Luxemburg involved herself – stemmed from the fact that the SPD was not opposing a bourgeois representative government, but, rather, a semi-absolutist police state.

It is important to understand the reactionary aristocratic climate in which social democracy was trying to develop. Two examples give a clear idea of how aristocrats saw themselves and the social democrats. In 1905, during the Morrocan crisis, Kaiser Wilhelm II wrote to the arch-reactionary Chancellor von Bülow:

> I cannot dispense with a single man at a moment when the social democracy preaches insurrection. We have first to shoot and behead the socialists and to render them innocuous – if necessary by a massacre – and then let's have war! But not before and not *a tempo*![8]

Indeed, as late as 1910, the ideology of divine right was still being employed. The following is from a public speech by Kaiser Wilhelm II:

> Here my grandfather placed the crown of Prussia on his head by his own right, and clearly pointed out that it had been given him solely by the grace of God, and not by parliaments, popular assemblies or decrees of the people,

27

and that he considered himself to be the chosen instrument of heaven . . . Considering myself to be the instrument of Him, without regard to any opinions or ideas, I proceed on my way.[9]

Because the German state took on the guise of constitutionalism but was actually still dominated by the aristocratic Junkers, the SPD was forced to advocate legislation that would allow the organisation of unions and help create bourgeois democratic institutions. Such legislation would enable the party to emerge from underground and avoid open persecution. In this regard, George Lichtheim is correct in claiming that it was democracy and the political demands for popular rule, rather than the calls for socio-economic reforms, which made the SPD a revolutionary threat to the prevailing order.[10]

Indeed, by 1890, Bismarck had already nationalised the railroads, set up a pioneering social security system, and formulated a welfare policy which included workmen's compensation. But all this occurred in the face of the growing underground SPD which, following Marx, sought to translate economic demands into political ones. The prevention of such a transformation was what Bismarck sought, and this created a concern for democracy among all segments of the party.

It was thus no accident that all of Rosa Luxemburg's opponents – and Luxemburg herself – agreed on the basic proposition that democracy could not be separated from socialism. The real differences within social democracy all centred around the concrete nature of this linkage. Thus, where Eduard Bernstein followed the road of parliamentary constitutionalism, and Kautsky that of republican democracy, for Rosa Luxemburg democracy was a process to be integrated into the everyday life of the proletariat. Indeed, the truly radical aspect of Rosa Luxemburg's thought is quintessentially political; democracy itself was to become the basic tool of proletarian education in socialism. Thus, it was she who took the bourgeois concept of democracy and attempted to extend it beyond formal, political representation into the realm of civil society.

The differences between the views of Bernstein, Kautsky, and Luxemburg – as well as the unanswered questions which they

28

raised – are still debated by the left. But it must be understood that, at the time, they continued to exist within a unique historical circumstance: socialist solidarity. The 'great debate' was carried on within the context of a socialist culture where the marxism of the *Erfurt Programme* prescribed a unity that transcended differences.

When a party is underground, the perception of the enemy and the assurance that justice is on the side of the oppressed and that victory will be achieved are central to the cohesion and elan of the movement. In this respect, the idea that a socialist victory was 'inevitable' played a fundamental ideological and political role. Its justification was to be found in the striking growth and success of the organisation which itself seemed to anticipate a socialist transformation of the existing order and the imminent collapse of capitalism. Such a belief did *not* create passivity as so many interpreters have suggested;[11] on the contrary, this belief and the 'science' of orthodox marxism spurred on the masses by fostering unity and new enthusiasm within a proletarian organisation which was fearful and exhausted since the Anti-Socialist laws had been lifted.[12]

It was the given complex of socio-historical conditions which dictated the form that marxism would take in Germany and within the Second International. Rather than serve as a critical method which would link means and ends, as well as develop alternative forms of social relations, marxism became an organisational dogma that ensured party unity and guaranteed the class base of its 'inevitable' victory. With the *Erfurt Programme* as its political expression, a programmatic expression in which revolutionary goals were split from immediate reforms, it was easy for marxism to become a revolutionary ideology that veiled a reformist practice.

This ideology was a fundamental constituent of party life when Rosa Luxemburg made her appearance on the social democratic stage. She was a member of the younger generation that had not gone through the period of the Anti-Socialist laws during which the thinking of the older German 'marxists', like Kautsky, Bebel and Liebknecht, had been formed.

Luxemburg recognised this herself and, while showing the old men respect, she felt that their time had passed. Thus, in

August of 1900, she wrote to the Kautskys that 'the *moral* loss resulting from (Wilhelm) Liebknecht's death is greater than you would initially care to think. The old generation passes and look what remains – God have mercy!' And yet, in the same letter, she goes on to say that Liebknecht 'died just in time to retain his fame.'[13] This letter manifests the ambivalence that Rosa Luxemburg came to experience in dealing with those older radicals who sponsored her in the face of what became the reformist challenge. Their support for her, however, was not unconnected with their need for allies in the struggle against the mounting threat from the right-wing of the party.

4. Revisionism and Orthodoxy

It was her participation in the 'revisionism debate' that thrust Rosa Luxemburg into the limelight of the international social democratic movement. The issues that would emerge were of importance from the start since the reformist challenge to orthodox marxism was already underway long before Eduard Bernstein wrote the series of articles that were to culminate in *Evolutionary Socialism*;[1] it was a practical challenge that manifested itself in the activities of figures such as Jaurès, Turati, Vollmar and the Fabians.

But, until the appearance of Bernstein's book, the attack upon marxism was never systematised. It was precisely the systematic character of Bernstein's attack which theoretically and programmatically crystallised a tendency that appealed to trade union leaders like Karl Legien, old Lassalleans, party bureaucrats, and even those 'marxists' who were sincerely convinced that the old theory had to be revised to meet a changed reality.

In Eduard Bernstein, these groupings found an extraordinary champion. A friend of Engels who had fled to Switzerland and then England in the face of anti-socialist persecution, a collaborator on the *Erfurt Programme* and a former editor of *Die Neue Zeit*, Bernstein had impeccable socialist credentials.[2] Furthermore, although many of his compatriots actually clung to a non-marxist worldview, Bernstein was himself convinced of the viability of socialism and thought that his revisionism was in the critical spirit of marxism. He saw the realisation of socialism as being 'evolutionary' rather than 'revolutionary' in its political manner precisely because, for him, the socio-economic conditions which Marx described no longer applied.

The socio-economic critique that he made was both

31

compact and incisive. In contrast to Marx – as interpreted by Kautsky and himself in the *Erfurt Programme* – Bernstein felt that he had uncovered trends that appeared to contradict the notion that capitalism was 'objectively and inevitably' doomed to destruction through the increasing wretchedness of the proletariat and the concentration of capital in fewer and fewer hands. Basing his observations roughly on the period of the Anti-Socialist laws, Bernstein noted that the middle class was on the rise and that medium sized firms were not falling by the wayside. This allowed him to conclude that the expected concentration of capital was not taking place and that the proletariat was not expanding. From his empirical analysis, Bernstein also argued that workers' wages were rising and that the extension of credit was overcoming crises in the business cycle. Because these objective socio-economic facts seemed to contradict Marx's predictions, Bernstein believed that the party had to come to terms with them in its theory. This, he claimed, it had already done in practice anyway since it was now following the course of a reformist trade union party. In short, Bernstein asked the SPD to alter its theory to fit its practice.

It is for this reason that even Karl Korsch praised Bernstein for expressing the reality of the SPD theoretically and charged his critics with misunderstanding Bernstein's project. Whatever the problems with Bernstein's position, Korsch felt that his book was 'the first serious attempt at a theoretical formulation of the actual ends and means of the bourgeois policy which [the SPD] actually practiced.'[3]

Under the circumstances, Bernstein thought it both useless and dishonest to maintain the revolutionary pretense. Insofar as the 'objective', 'economic' basis for capitalism's 'inevitable collapse' was being undermined by socio-economic reality, he felt that it was dangerous to keep talking about a revolutionary goal. Such talk would scare away those middle strata which – in his view – were essential for the electoral success of the SPD. Still, Bernstein did believe that socialism was desirable as a means of redistributing income and ensuring parliamentary government within the terms of representative democracy. But, from the standpoint of 'orthodox' marxists, this meant that the creation of socialism was grounded on nothing other than an ethical

32

demand. Indeed, it is not surprising that Bernstein should later flirt with Kant to substantiate his political orientation philosophically. Because social conditions were improving, because it was useless to argue about the goal and because the SPD was bringing socialism about in practice anyway, Bernstein could make his famous statement that 'the movement is everything and the goal is nothing'.

It is difficult to understand today how deeply Bernstein's theory shook the socialist world. The marxist theory that had sustained the workers' movement during the long arduous years of underground work and growth was being attacked at its very core, and the erupting storm involved Bebel, Kautsky, Plekhanov and others in the defense of marxism. It was, however, Luxemburg's *Social Reform or Revolution* that was the most penetrating critique of Bernstein's position and that remains one of her most relevant works today. Luxemburg tackles revisionism head on and draws the practical political conclusions. She makes the telling observation that it is not a question of revisionism defending capitalist relations *per se*. For:

> its theory is based on the presupposition of the existence of these contradictions, just like the marxist conception. But, on the other hand, what constitutes precisely the essential kernel of revisionism and distinguishes it fundamentally from the attitude taken by social democracy up to now is that it does not base its theory on the suppression of these contradictions as a result of their logical internal development. The theory of revisionism occupies an intermediate place between two extremes. Revisionism does not want to see the contradictions of capitalism mature, [nor to] suppress these contradictions through a revolutionary transformation. Rather, it wants to lessen, to attenuate the capitalist contradictions.[5]

The contradictions are attenuated by the particular 'socialist' reforms that the existing system accepts. For this very reason, reformists equate socialism with the reforms that are achieved under capitalism. It is this implicit assumption by reformists which is the key to the revisionism debate and to contemporary social democracy as well.

For Luxemburg, it was not merely the particular abuses of capitalism, but rather the relations of capitalism as a whole that needed to be transformed. As a dialectician she fully understood that structural transformation could not be divorced from those reforms which build the consciousness and ease the burden of the working class. Instead, the necessities of the goal must inform the practical reforms that are to be undertaken by the working class and serve as a guide for what is to be supported and what is to be opposed. Thus, in immediately practical terms, a choice confronted the working class over the question of militarism.[6] The reformist, Max Schippel, suggested that it was necessary for the SPD to support the development of a German navy; this, along with support for military build-up, would obviously prime the economy and create jobs for workers. From Luxemburg's standpoint, however, not only would this fuel nationalism and so undermine the long-term international goals of socialism: it would also strengthen the state which socialists should seek to overthrow. By the same token, she sought to emphasise radical demands which were not technically in the party platform – such as the call for a republic – in order to build the *revolutionary* consciousness of the working class and prepare it for the fundamental crises that would emerge.[7]

This demand for the practical anticipation of crises was necessitated by Luxemburg's claim, in opposition to Bernstein, that credit does not reduce the potential for crisis, but exacerbates it.[8] Indeed, what would become prominent in her underconsumption thesis in *The Accumulation of Capital* already appears in her controversy with Bernstein: that crises do not emerge from shrinkage in the capitalist economy, but rather from periods of great expansion[9] which themselves affect the growth of the working class positively. Rosa Luxemburg argued that Bernstein completely misunderstood Marx's theory of the centralisation of capital by mechanistically and empirically looking for the disappearance of small businesses in relation to the rise of large scale capitalist enterprise.[10] In her view, the potential for crisis continued to exist and there can be little question that in the following years the attenuation of crises did not occur; the depressions of 1918–1924 and 1929–32 alone support this standpoint.

But, the economic argument is truly relevant only when the

political consequences are extracted from the analysis. Therefore, it is essential to note how Luxemburg exposed the optimistic and unsupported presuppositions that Bernstein had made regarding the possibilities for the evolution of socialism within a stabilised capitalism. Because of his long exile in England, Bernstein assumed the existence of democracy as an arena for socialist reform. Extrapolating from the English situation, Bernstein believed that the rapid growth of German social democracy combined with the attenuation of economic crises would create the conditions in which socialism could peacefully grow over time. Indeed, like Kautsky and many other marxists of his generation, Bernstein retained a linear view of historical progress which implied that democracy evolved with the development of capitalism.[11] But, Luxemburg reminded her audience, there was no intrinsic relation between capitalism and even the crudest parliamentary democracy and the economic system of capitalism could exist with any number of political forms.[12]

From the first Luxemburg recognised the value of democratic forms in the transformation of capitalism. But, parliamentarism manifested a contradictory tendency that had to be taken into account:

> Precisely its form serves parliamentarism to express, within the organisation of the state, the interests of the whole of society. But, on the other hand, what parliamentarism expresses here is still capitalist society, that is to say, a society in which *capitalist* interests are still dominant – and it is these which parliamentarism expresses.[13]

Given this contradiction, it becomes clear that without the 'goal' of a socialist society the SPD would not only accept the values of a repressive bourgeois society implicitly, but would also eventually turn into a bourgeois parliamentary party inasmuch as it would be ideologically integrated into the existing structure. Luxemburg saw that there is a relation between means and ends; that the disavowal of its *raison d'etre* would affect the character of the party:

> The difference is not in the *what* but in the *how*. At present,

35

the trade union and the parliamentary struggles are considered as means of gradually guiding and educating the proletariat for the taking of political power. From the revisionist standpoint, this conquest of power is impossible and useless; therefore, trade union and parliamentary activity are to be carried on only for their immediate results, that is, the bettering of the material situation of the workers, the gradual reduction of capitalist exploitation and the extension of social control . . . The most probable immediate result of this is, then, a tactical shift toward using all means to make possible the practical results, the social reforms. As soon as immediate, practical results become the principal aim, the clear-cut, irreconcilable class standpoint, which has meaning only insofar as it proposes to take power, will be found more and more an obstacle. The direct consequence of this will be the adoption by the Party of a 'policy of compensation', a policy of horse-trading, and an attitude of diplomatic conciliation.[14]

So, it would be just as serious a mistake to believe that Rosa Luxemburg carried on her polemic simply to justify marxism theoretically as it would to assume that she accepted the political practice of the SPD uncritically. She saw the debate in practical political terms which involved the fundamental political orientation of social democracy itself.

Reformism was not something which arbitrarily came into existence, but a tendency inherent in any socialist movement:

Legal reform and revolution are not different methods of historical progress that can be picked out at pleasure from the counter of history, just as one chooses hot or cold sausages. They are different *moments* in the development of class society which condition and complement each other, and at the same time exclude each other reciprocally . . . In the history of classes, revolution is the act of political creation while legislation is the political expression of the life of a society that has already come into being. Work for legal reforms does not contain its own driving force independent from revolution. During every historical period, work for reforms is carried on only in the direction given it by the impetus of the last revolution, and continues as long as that impulsion continues to make itself felt.[15]

From this perspective, it is impossible to equate socialism with the particular reforms that are achieved and 'absolutely false and totally unhistorical to represent the work for reforms as a drawn-out revolution, and revolution as a condensed series of reforms.'[16] The fact that this debate occurred within a political context of assumed unity limited the range of her critique. But, the conclusion is clear. If the results of reformist practice cannot be identified with revolution, then a fundamental strategic cleavage exists within the Party that cannot be ignored. For, 'whoever pronounces themselves in favour of the method of legal reforms *in place of and as opposed to* the conquest of political power and social revolution does not really choose a tranquil, surer and slower road to the *same* goal. They choose a *different* goal.'[17]

In this light, her somewhat tempered suggestions that the Party could exist without Bernstein make sense. It also becomes clear what Luxemburg meant by her statement that it is only the goal which separates the SPD from all other parties; to give up the emphasis upon this revolutionary goal would ultimately result in the surrender of radical reforms as well.[18]

Thus, when Luxemburg argued for the primary importance of the goal, she was actually arguing that the SPD must look to its revolutionary theory – as elaborated in the *Erfurt Programme* – to inform and radicalise its practice precisely in order to ensure its continued success.

> In effect, our programme would be a miserable scrap of paper if it could not serve us in *all* eventualities, at *all* moments of the struggle, and serve precisely by its *application* and not by its nonapplication. If our programme is the formulation of the historical development of society from capitalism to socialism, obviously it must also formulate, in all their fundamental lines, all the transitory phases of this development, and consequently at *every* moment it should be able to indicate to the proletariat what ought to be correct behaviour in order to move toward socialism. It follows generally that there can be *no time*

37

when the proletariat will be obliged to abandon its programme, or be abandoned by it.[19]

Through such remarks, Rosa Luxemburg could appear as an ally of both Bebel and Kautsky in the controversy. Indeed, tactically, Luxemburg's argument put her in the position where she could say:

> There is no opposition from the left in the party, there is only an opposition from the right. As a whole, the party stands where it has always stood: on *our* side. In the opposition to the party, there are only comrades inclined toward opportunism who are committed only to 'practical politics'.[20]

Abstract theory always meant very little to Rosa Luxemburg. What concerned her was the increasing dominance of reformist practice within the Second International. To creeping parliamentarism was added increasing reliance upon the trade unions, especially in Germany. It was not that Luxemburg rejected the trade union movement out of hand. She recognised that it could influence the apportionment of labour, the amount of wages, and potentially even the price of goods.[21] But, she also saw that the emphasis upon immediate reforms would displace the revolutionary consciousness necessary for the political seizure of power by the working class. This consciousness would also be endangered by separating economic demands from political ones. Indeed, the trade union vision of change in terms of discrete reforms threatened the perception of the 'totality' and so opened the way to bourgeois ideology.

For these reasons, and also because Luxemburg realised that it was the political demands of social democracy that constituted the real threat to the given order, she saw that trade union reformism harboured the probability of integration into the established system. Luxemburg viewed trade union activity in 'defensive' terms and denied that the unions could control either the actual level of wages or the production process in a bourgeois state.[22] Because the unions did not question the socio-political *system* of capitalist exploitation, Luxemburg termed their work a 'labour of Sisyphus'[23] – a remark which earned her their undying hatred. This would ultimately be of great significance when the bulk of the trade union leadership proved instrumental in opposing the socialist left during the 1918 revolt.

But Rosa Luxemburg won her battle with the revisionists, at least formally, when the SPD overwhelmingly rejected the Bernsteinian heresy in 1899. This, however, had little to do with the vigour of her arguments *per se*. Indeed, in political terms, the value of the orthodox ideology had been proven while the extraordinary class divisions that still remained rendered the debate over the relative – as against the absolute – impoverishment of the working class practically superfluous.[24] However, the reactionary policies pursued by Kaiser Wilhelm II and the support that they were accorded by the broader middle strata only seemed to ensure the isolation of the SPD. In short:

> It is hard to see what the party would have gained if it had renounced [its] belief, abandoned its marxism, disavowed the class struggle, repudiated revolution and followed Bernstein in declaring itself a 'party of democratic socialist reform' – a party for which 'the movement is everything, the aim nothing'. It is not even likely that, by thus compromising its ideology and tactics, it would have gained more in the way of social reform for the working class, and it would certainly have done nothing to extend democratic rights. Whatever language the party might choose to speak, Prussia would not have altered her electoral system, and Germany would not have turned herself into a parliamentary democracy on the British pattern. But, by abandoning the faith in its great historical mission which marxism gave to the working class, the roots of enthusiasm, which were the source of so much vitality in the social democratic movement, would surely have withered. Moreover, such 'loss of faith' would undoubtedly have destroyed the unity of the party and weakened the working class to a disasterous extent.[25]

Yet, if Luxemburg recognised the strength of the revisionist current from the start and was critical and aware of reformism's strength within the party, then why did she join the social democratic movement in the first place? After all, there were other groups that she could have joined; there were anarchist organisations, and even an ultra-left group called *Die Jungen* (The Young Ones), whose members included Gustav Landauer and Johann Most, that had been purged from the SPD.

The simplicity of the answer to this question should not obscure its importance. Rosa Luxemburg knew that 'a correct line' was not within the reach of a party that was cut off from the masses. 'Staying in contact with the masses' was the political motto that she followed to the end of her life. Small sectarian movements meant nothing to her and 'splitting' the workers movement was always suspect. Luxemburg recognised that, given the existence of a mass workers' party, it was easier to be right in theory while sitting in a cafe than attempting to come to terms with the exigencies of existing political practice. This was what led her to say that a mistake the workers make in their own actions, from which they learn, is worth more than ten victories won under the guidance of the wisest central committee.

Though, in Luxemburg's view, a mass organisation was necessary for this learning process to be effective, this stance led her to be criticised by conservative social democrats and Bolsheviks alike for believing in a 'spontaneity thesis'. Luxemburg, was not a narrow spontaneist. Yet, her refusal to subordinate the interests of the class to those of the party, her willingness to recognise that socialism cannot be realised by decree, and her attempt to develop a dialectical relation between party and mass, would ultimately pit Rosa Luxemburg against all forms of organisational dogmatism and give her a unique position in the development of socialist thought.

5. Intermezzo: Rosa Luxemburg and the Cultural Milieu of Social Democracy

Many people assume that radical politics necessarily engender radical tastes in art. This assumption is certainly not valid in the case of Rosa Luxemburg. Although she stood on the far left of the Second International, Luxemburg's cultural tastes were very much in accordance with the views that were dominant among the intellectuals of the international social democratic movement.

Those who were more modern favoured the naturalistic and realistic in a work of art. But, there was also a concern with classicism and romanticism.[1] Following the predilections of Marx and Engels, the emphasis was clearly on the elaboration of the cultural heritage of the revolutionary bourgeoisie.

Marxist cultural criticism was still in its infancy during the years of the Second International. Both the Stalinist excesses of 'socialist realism' as well as the experimentalist-modernist views that would flower in the twenties and thirties with Ernst Bloch, Walter Benjamin, Brecht and even Trotsky, were still virtually unknown to the socialist reading public.

As far as the mainstream of the SPD was concerned, theoretical aesthetics was of secondary importance. Directly political and social issues were seen as more pressing. The first order of priority when it came to culture involved giving the workers access to those cultural goods which only the ruling classes had the time and money to enjoy. Furthermore, it was believed that the bourgeoisie had stopped playing a progressive role and that – as in the political realm – the capitalists had betrayed the revolutionary ideals of their own cultural representatives such as the great writers of the French Enlightenment as well as Lessing, Schiller, and Goethe. In the cultural realm, as in the political sphere, the SPD found it necessary to re-establish the revolutionary democratic and humanistic values of the bourgeoisie with regard to the goals of the working class.

41

It was this context that produced the two dominant literary figures of the Second International: Franz Mehring and Georgii Plekhanov. Rosa Luxemburg knew both of them, and her continual references to Mehring's masterpiece of literary criticism, *The Lessing Legend*, come as no surprise.[2] As with so many socialist thinkers who are now, unfortunately, virtually forgotten Mehring and Plekhanov were remarkable individuals. Mehring – the author of the great biography *Karl Marx*, for which Rosa Luxemburg wrote the economics chapter – was also an important polemicist and later a co-founder of the Spartacus League; Plekhanov, a towering intellect, was a major theorist – his works include *Fundamental Problems of Marxism* – and came to be known as Lenin's early mentor as well as the 'father of Russian marxism'.

Both Mehring and Plekhanov were socialists whose literary values were derived from the Enlightenment. Both were rationalists and both were sociological in their approach to art which they considered in terms of the class relations it mirrored and the possibility it offered for education in the broadest sense. It is no accident then that neither Mehring nor Plekhanov (nor indeed Luxemburg) valued the avant-grade movements that were developing around the turn of the century such as Art Nouveau, Fauvism, Futurism, Expressionism and so on. For all those movements unleashed their aesthetic fury upon the classical-rationalist bourgeois past and were essentially confined to the bohemian literati until shortly before the outbreak of World War I.[3]

Such were the social democratic attitudes that fundamentally coloured Rosa Luxemburg's aesthetic perspective. The two basic elements of this outlook were: the pedagogic social content and the expression of the individual's inner experience. Alone neither was sufficient, and the emphasis that she placed upon one or the other in the particular context was simply that – a matter of emphasis. The social aspect naturally assumed greater primacy in the few aesthetic pieces that she wrote for popular consumption. Yet, when she wrote about Romain Rolland's *Jean-Christophe in Paris* in one of her letters, she said that despite its progressive political message and naturalist form: 'It is not an authentic work of art. I am so inexorably sensitive in these matters that even the most beautiful (political) tendency cannot substitute for God-given genius.'[4]

Rosa Luxemburg was not particularly influenced by the SPD's attempts to create a 'popular' workers' culture. Rather, she drew a line between art and propaganda. Indeed, as becomes clear in her essay, 'Tolstoy as a Social Thinker',[5] the value of the great artist does not lie in the positive propagandist solutions that are held out for the future, but rather in the depth of the author's criticism of existing society. Rosa Luxemburg is therefore quite removed from the Stalinist method of first identifying the work of art with the politics it professes and then judging its value.[6] Still, in the beautiful introduction to her translation of Korolenko's *History of My Contemporary*, she noted how the Russian literary tradition 'was born out of opposition to the Russian regime, out of the spirit of struggle'.[7]

By the same token, Luxemburg criticised Baudelaire, Wedekind, and D'Annunzio for their 'egotism' and their 'over-saturation with modern culture'.[8] The reasons are self-evident: for Rosa Luxemburg, although the experience of art might enrapture the individual, it had also to edify personal development and social views. Thus, a moralistic element that sometimes verges on the puritanical enters her observations – this is also in accord with the dominant attitudes of socialists at the turn of the century.

Social democracy saw itself as the wave of the future and as a movement that was preserved from the decadence of bourgeois society. This theme, which Kautsky and others emphasised so consistently, also runs through Rosa Luxemburg's letters, and it is fascinating to see how it influences her aesthetic judgments. Thus, she could criticise Titian for being too elegant, Hölderlin for being 'too stately', and even the much admired and extremely popular Ricarda Huch for an occasional lack of feminine modesty.

In this sense, it is also no wonder that Rosa Luxemburg should look to the important romantic Eduard Mörike, whose lyrical, often overly sentimental poetry purifies nature. In fact, it becomes obvious that for her the romantic complements the naturalist-realist worldview. The experience of transcendent rapture – which is fundamental to romanticism – is often seen as

43

inimically opposed to a naturalism that brings the individual face to face with the decadence and misery of human interaction in a given system. What unites the two modes, however, is the unmediated character of the subject's relation to the external world. The romantic impulse, a concern with nature and the refinement of the emotions provide a certain insight into the peace and serenity for which Rosa Luxemburg personally longed. On the other hand, the harsh reality that has to be overcome is elucidated in the realist form.

Rosa Luxemburg never linked the two aesthetic modes together and seemed to oscillate back and forth between them. For where she demanded the subjective emotional experience of reality basic to romanticism, she also called for an objectively realistic quality along with a comprehension of repression within the social realm that is fostered by naturalism and realism.

Luxemburg never sought to reconcile the contradiction between these two aesthetic views, or to enquire into the nature of artistic transcendence. For her, a work continually assumed validity in the present. The sculptures of Rodin strike her on account of their humanism, on account of their dignity – and she immediately thinks of her fellow member of the International and opponent Jaurès. Or take Voltaire: before the war he had little meaning for her; his *Candide*, a 'wicked compilation of all human vices', originally struck her as a caricature of the human condition – but when the war was unleashed it became 'totally realistic'.[9]

There is hardly a work which she praises that is not considered in the context of its immediate relevance. Nevertheless, the immediacy that she prized was fundamentally different from the immediacy that was essential to the avant-garde of her time and which has become part and parcel of the modern novel. The singular concern with the subject to the exclusion of the external world, the employment of shock and the existential emphasis upon '*Angst*' as the authentic moment in which reality is laid bare – all go against the grain of Luxemburg's aesthetic tastes and those of the Second International as a whole.

For these socialists, literature involved more than an examination of what has been called the 'new inwardness'. But, in Luxemburg's view neither was art simply a vehicle for an

44

author's contempt of the prevalent forms of social interaction. This becomes clear in a discussion of Galsworthy in one of her letters,[10] and it provides a valuable insight into her own values. Though she found Galsworthy 'brilliant' after reading *The Man of Property* her opinion changes with *Fraternity*. In the latter work, Galsworthy is seen as too 'sophisticated', and Luxemburg compares him to Shaw and Wilde.

Obviously, Luxemburg was put off by this peculiarly English mode of cynical, 'civilised' and 'cultured' social criticism. She believed that this type of criticism, which manifests itself with the three authors in question, marked the ideological decadence of bourgeois culture at the turn of the century. Despite the good humour and the progressive social consciousness – which she fully appreciated – the comedy of manners still leaves the social realm untouched as it points up hypocrisy.

Irony, naturally, is at the centre of this form. And it is just the element of ironic cynicism that preserves the status quo insofar as the author alone achieves exemption from the hypocritical frailties of which he accuses society at large. Since everyone except the author is caught in the mire of hypocrisy, there is no possibility for locating the basis of a solidarity that would transform the status quo. Thus, a cynical egotism undermines the possibility of social transformation and happiness.

Luxemburg's concern for happiness is part of her own *joie de vivre*, and it marks the way in which she experienced literature. Thus, she could agree with her beloved Korolenko's simple statement: 'Happiness is salubrious and elevating to the soul. And I always believe, you know, that man is rather obliged to be happy'.[11] This is a demand that art project its 'promesse de bonheur' (Stendhal), which does not mean that it is simply an 'expedient luxury for releasing the feelings of beauty, or happiness, in beautiful souls'. The liberating potential within art is not there for an elite, but – as the socialists realised – for the masses who can be taught to recognise it. Art is not passive, but rather becomes part of the struggle against oppression.

As with many of her comrades, Luxemburg's literary interests became part of the response to the oppression which she endured during her confinements in prison. Not only was she able to retain some sense of social interaction through art, but the emotive experience itself became crucial insofar as it enabled her to come to grips with her isolation. Sitting in a tiny cell, she would recite her Mörike in the dark. It wasn't much, but the stimulus to the imagination that his poetry provided helped keep her will to liberation alive.

Particularly in prison, Rosa Luxemburg revelled in what Walter Benjamin would later call the 'aura' of a work of art. Rosa, herself, employed no categories; art was simply a way of gaining a breadth of knowledge and an emotive exaltation. Neither in her letters nor her essays did she seek to reflect upon the nature of the aesthetic experience or the epistemological categories that allow for the understanding of that experience.

In this regard, she was no different from most of her socialist contemporaries. She thought very little of 'literary criticism' as such. For criticism, at the time, was still essentially the preserve of bohemia – as in the case of Valéry or Mallarmé – and the university which in Germany was strongly dominated by the influence of Dilthey and the neo-Kantians.

Luxemburg and her comrades did not generally look to the complex or the innovative in cultural matters. The names that consistently appear in her letters are the ones common to the period. In fact, if there is something striking in her correspondence regarding the turn-of-the-century cultural milieu of socialism, it is not the inclusion of certain names but the omission of certain others. There is virtually no mention of reactionary or proto-fascist writers, like Claudel or Barrés, who would exert such an enormous influence. At the same time, artists like Gide or Thomas Mann, who were to influence the cultural production of the future fundamentally, hardly appear; nor is there any discussion of painters like Cezanne, Matisse, Klee or Kandinsky.

In the case of Luxemburg, these lapses were clearly self-induced; her friend Franz Pfemfert, the editor of the expressionist organ *Die Aktion* (Action), would surely have tried to introduce her to the important works of modernism. But, in accordance with the prevailing cultural attitudes of social democracy, Rosa Luxemburg shied away. Thus, in one of her letters, she stated:

I don't understand [Hugo von] Hofmannsthal, and I don't know [Stefan] George. It's true: with all of them, I am a bit frightened of their complete mastery of form, by their poetic means of expression, and their lack of a grand noble *Weltanschauung*.[12]

From an early limited flirtation with avant-gardists like Richard Dehmel, Arno Holz and Johann Schlaf, Rosa Luxemburg retreated to Mörike and Goethe, to the terrain upon which she and her socialist contemporaries felt secure.

Certain critics, like J. P. Nettl, have chosen to regard Rosa Luxemburg's opposition to the avant-garde as somehow precipitating of the marxist theory of realism whose primary exponent would be Georg Lukacs. To emphasise her role in this regard, however, is to stretch a point. It is not simply a question of her opposing modernism – Goethe had already done that in his time, and more self-consciously – nor is it a question of her being more tolerant than Lukacs in her aesthetic judgments, or more eclectic. What becomes essential is that the categories upon which a marxist aesthetic can be based are missing in her observations. Unlike Lukacs, for example, Rosa Luxemburg never actually described the concrete content of this 'grand, noble *Weltanschauung*' which is lacking in the modernists. Moreover, she does not draw any structural differentiations between writers as different as Galsworthy and Tolstoy, or even Mörike and Goethe.

Rosa Luxemburg did not feel the need for any systematic theory of aesthetics. The criteria which she used were often arbitrary; they involved little more than her personal perception of emotional and social needs. Thus Rosa Luxemburg was not a real influence on marxist aesthetics. Her aesthetic limitations were the limitations of her age and contemporaries. The theories that would seek to interpret art in terms of its liberating possibilities would have to await the Hegelian revival within marxism, the ideological degeneration of the major socialist parties and to some extent the displacement of revolution from the political into the cultural realm.

Yet, even here, Luxemburg has something to offer. For she truly loved literature and there was nothing doctrinaire in her

47

attitudes towards it. She never simply reduced the artistic to the political, nor did she ever try to force art into pre-defined trans-historical categories. Indeed, Luxemburg understood that art has a purpose; that art should dignify the possibilities of human existence as it exposes real misery, that art should expand the imagination and build the humanistic values of co-operation and solidarity as it shows how they are denied. Perhaps there is a certain naivety in her views, but there is also a certain wisdom and vigour. The values she brought to art were those that she brought to life. This allowed her to write: 'In theoretical work, as in art, I value only the simple, the tranquil and the bold'. For her, that was enough.

6. The East European Dimension

Few individuals rose to fame in the socialist world as quickly as Rosa Luxemburg. Still, she had to earn her spurs as a party worker and so, in 1898, the SPD sent her to Poznan. There, at the 'boundary between civilisation and barbarism',[1] she attempted to organise the Polish migrant and settler workers. Travelling in the area proved exhausting, the incessant meetings tiring and the organisational work mundane. But in this work Luxemburg gained the practical experience that enabled her to become the party's expert on east European questions, and its delegate to the International. Her experience also led her to be chosen to sit on the commission that was to arbitrate the bitter quarrel that had broken out between the Bolsheviks and Mensheviks in 1902.

Tension had existed within the Russian Social Democratic Party since its formation in 1898. On the one hand, there were those who wished to follow the political lead of their European socialist comrades. These individuals desired a democratic mass-based socialist movement. But, due to the backward nature of Russian social conditions, they believed that, in the interim, the working class must follow the political initiatives of the bourgeoisie while emphasising trade union activity within the framework of Russian economic development. On the other hand, there were those who believed that the proletariat could not simply follow the political lead of the bourgeoisie. They advocated the creation of a revolutionary proletarian class consciousness by stressing the need for an autonomous political organisation of the working class which would also get support from the oppressed peasantry.[2] Most 'orthodox' marxists supported the 'economist' view that Russia's coming revolution must be bourgeois and that the proletariat would only have a secondary role. Lenin became the leader of the younger and more political faction that opposed such 'econom-

49

ism' and which adhered to a more Jacobin conception of revolution with its emphasis upon an elite 'vanguard'.

For her part, Rosa Luxemburg tried to emphasise the need for unity between the two factions after the split. Yet, as this hope diminished, it emerges clearly from her actions and letters that, despite the ambivalent feelings which she held about Lenin and her dislike of the arrogance as well as the intrigues of the Bolsheviks, she drew ever further away from the Mensheviks who ultimately became champions of the Polish Socialist Party.[3] Of course, Luxemburg's support for the Bolsheviks was never uncritical. Yet, however much she disagreed with Lenin, there was one decisive point on which they were in theoretical agreement – the trade unions.

Already in 1903, in his now famous *What Is To Be Done?*, Lenin had argued that trade union consciousness could never be anything other than reformist. From Lenin's standpoint, the emphasis upon economic reform – to the detriment of political action – could not create a revolutionary consciousness amongst the working class since such consciousness requires the translation of economic demands into political ones. Luxemburg also saw the need for such a translation, and Lenin's view of the trade unions converges with her own notion of the 'defensive' nature of trade union activity. Both saw the need for a party to assert its control over the trade unions and the 'labour aristocracy', but Lenin was to draw different conclusions regarding the character of the party itself and its relation to the masses.

Given the inability of the trade unions to create revolutionary consciousness, Lenin argued for a revolutionary 'vanguard' party, composed of a relatively small number of dedicated revolutionary intellectuals who would inject the required revolutionary consciousness 'from without'. For Lenin, it is the party which alone incarnates the 'true' class consciousness of the workers. Political decisions would therefore be the preserve of the party alone while the guiding organisational rule to create the necessary discipline within the party would be 'democratic centralism' – though an individual might dissent from a party decision in private, he or she had to support that decision in public.

In this regard, Lenin differed from his other famous comrades in the Russian Social Democratic Party – Plekhanov, Martov and Trotsky – as well as from most European socialists. But Lenin's position was perhaps logical in Russia given the semi-absolutist Tsarist state, the absence of a working class tradition, marxist theory, a 'mass party' organisation and a powerful trade union movement.

When Lenin's *What Is To Be Done?* first appeared, it caused very little fuss in the west. Indeed, it was only translated into German in the twenties. Part of the reason was that the entire controversy seemed to be a tempest in a teapot; a faction fight within a weak party organisation that reflected the backwardness of the very society that had to be overcome. Another reason lay in the fact that the question over the party's character seemed only to involve a matter of degree rather than kind. After all, the German party leadership, well known for its power and the demands it made on party discipline, was also composed of 'revolutionary intellectuals'. Finally, at the time, Lenin's desire for a mass base as well as his respect for democracy, a republic, and Kautskyan theory, seemed unshakeable.

But very early on, Rosa Luxemburg saw the importance of Lenin's statement. Her response to it and to Lenin's *One Step Forward, Two Steps Back* (1904) occurs in one of her most important essays, 'Organizational Questions of Social Democracy'.

Here, the emphasis falls upon the need for a mass party. From the first, Luxemburg makes clear that there is *necessarily*

> a strong tendency toward centralism inherent in social democracy. Social democracy grows in the economic soil of capitalism, which itself tends toward centralism. Its struggle occurs within the political framework of the large, centralised bourgeois state. Further, social democracy is fundamentally an outspoken opponent of every particularism and national federalism. It is called upon to represent, within the framework of a given state, the totality of the interests of the proletariat as a class, as opposed to all partial and group interests. Therefore, it follows that social democracy has the natural aspiration of welding together all national, religious, and professional groups of the working class into a unified party.[4]

Along with Kautsky, and in contrast to so many 'scientific'

51

marxists who continually speak of 'class' in economistic terms and who throw up their hands in despair at the occupational splits that they uncover within the working class, Luxemburg understood that the *constitution* of a *revolutionary* working class must be seen in fundamentally *political* terms: it is the very *raison d'etre* of the party to unify the seemingly 'objectively' differentiated strata of the working class into a cohesive class that exists 'in-itself and for-itself.'

The question is not whether a party should exist, or even whether the spontaneity of the masses should be considered primary. The real question for Luxemburg is how to establish the conceptual *relation* between party and mass with regard to the revolutionary goal to be achieved: the self-administration of the working class.

But, the realisation of this goal starts in 'the elementary class struggle' that points out, politically, the structural contradictions within capitalism while advocating specific measures of reform. Between revolution and reform, spontaneity and organisation, the class politics of social democracy:

> thus move in the dialectical contradiction that here the proletarian army is first recruited in the struggle itself, and that only in the struggle does it become aware of the objectives of the struggle. Here, organisation, enlightenment and struggle are not separate mechanically and temporally different moments, as is the case with a Blanquist movement. Here they are only different sides of the same process.[5]

Consequently, although the differences between Luxemburg and Lenin's views on the relation between party and mass can be exaggerated, Luxemburg did not accept the idea that consciousness can be manufactured and then injected into the masses from the outside. Instead, class consciousness emerges from the interaction between a party that draws out the revolutionary demands of its membership and a mass membership whose needs can become articulated in the party through public discussion.

Precisely because the working class must transform itself from 'dead machines' into the 'free and independent directors' of

52

society as a whole, the working class must learn what it needs to know and have the opportunity to exercise its knowledge. In Luxemburg's view, this must be institutionally guaranteed and it is this which becomes the role of the party. Consequently, contrary to what Lenin believed, it follows that:

> the social democratic centralisation cannot be based on blind obedience, nor on the mechanical subordination of the party militants to a central power. On the other hand, it follows that an absolute dividing wall cannot be erected between the class-conscious kernel of the proletariat, already organised as a party cadre, and the immediate popular environment which is gripped by the class struggle and finds itself in the process of class enlightenment.[6]

The real issue here is democracy, both inside and outside the party, for only in this way can the consistent interaction between party and mass be assured. Luxemburg also believes that the 'class conscious kernel' of the working class must retain its revolutionary perspective. But without the willingness to debate, to criticise, to reach the disparate interests of the masses through public dialogue, the revolutionary means turn against the revolutionary end. Thus, in criticising the growing petrification within the trade union movement, she wrote that:

> Through the concentration of the strings of the movement in its hands, the capacity of judging in trade union affairs becomes its professional specialty. The mass of comrades are degraded to a mass incapable of judging, whose essential virtue becomes 'discipline', that is, passive obedience to duty.[7]

This is the same critique she would later level against the Bolsheviks as well as her own German Social Democratic Party. Where the party can, and must, seek to *influence* the masses – by formulating a programme and carrying on with revolutionary agitation in periods of lull – it should not have the arrogance to *rule* them. It is in the forging of a unity between spontaneity and organisation that the political maturity of the class will develop; active recognition of the moment when the working class can realise its own possibilities is the goal, but such action must itself be organised in such a way that these possibilities are extended

53

and clarified in revolutionary terms. The party must therefore necessarily play a *pedagogic* role. What ultimately results from Luxemburg's vision is a party organisation that will educate its membership practically so that its own power can be transferred to the masses themselves.

It is foolish to argue that Luxemburg ignored the growth, or potential growth, of reformist elements within the party; nor is it correct to assess her view as 'objectivistic', seeing the quick development of a unified class consciousness stemming from a purely economic basis.[8] As the ossification of the SPD apparatus grew, Luxemburg continually attempted to fight within the party and simultaneously directed her appeals to the membership itself. From the first, however, she never simply narrowed her concerns to fit those of the industrial workers; rather, she sought to unite the oppressed in terms of a broad class framework that would oppose the capitalist system. In this way, a political problem presents itself which:

> lies in the essence of social democratic struggle itself, in its internal contradictions. The world-historical advance of the proletariat to its victory is a process whose particularity lies in the fact that here, for the first time in history, the masses of the people themselves are expressing their will against all ruling classes. But this will can only be realised outside and beyond present society. On the other hand, this will can only develop in the daily struggle with the established order, thus, only within its framework. The unification of the great mass of the people with a goal that goes beyond the whole established order, of the daily struggle with the revolutionary overthrow – this is the dialectical contradiction of the social democratic movement which must develop consistently between two obstacles: the loss of its mass character and the abandonment of its goal, becoming a sect and becoming a bourgeois reformist movement.[9]

What emerges here is the fundamental contradiction between the bureaucratic needs of political organisation and the necessity of forging the working class's aspirations to self-administration. This contradiction lies within both social democratic and Euro-

Communist parties alike and neither element of it can afford to be ignored if the questions of state power, centralisation and decentralisation, multi-nationals, internationalism and programme are to be formulated in an emancipatory fashion.

The result of Luxemburg's analysis is the framework for an alternative, which undermines the usual criticism that the relation which she posits between the *moments* of 'organisation, enlightenment and struggle', is not specified. Such a relation can never be articulated *a priori* if the analysis is to avoid the worst forms of mechanistic marxism and dogmatism. The actual relation between these moments must arise from the specific situation itself in its possibilities for the working class.

This it did in 1905, the year in which she was to elaborate her position on the 'mass strike'. It must be understood from the start, however, that Rosa Luxemburg did not invent the theory of the mass strike; it had long been the central concern of the anarcho-syndicalists. Indeed it was not even she, but Parvus, who originally formulated the mass strike theory in marxist terms. What clearly differentiated her theory of the strike was its development as a *process*. The year 1905 – which is usually seen as marking the beginning of the mass strike revolt in Russia – was itself the culmination of an earlier movement. In 1902, a wave of strikes had hit Batum. In December of that year the strikes spread to Rostov-on-Don, and 1903 saw widespread strikes break out first in Baku and then in Tiflis, Odessa, Kiev and other cities. It was in 1905 that the strike of one hundred and forty thousand workers resulted in the creation of the St. Petersberg Soviet, which elected the youthful Trotsky as its president.

These events marked the shift of revolutionary consciousness from the advanced proletariat of western Europe to a backward Russia. News spread slowly to the west, but when it finally came it struck like a thunderbolt. In 1905, when August Bebel brought the matter up for discussion at the SPD conference in Jena, Luxemburg took the most radical stance in support of this revolutionary experiment in proletarian rule. Interestingly enough in opposition to trade union representatives like Karl Legien and Theodor Bomelberg who felt that support for such a venture would threaten the work of decades, she received the backing of reformists like Eduard Bernstein and Kurt Eisner who felt that the mass strike could be used to win universal suffrage in Prussia as it was being used in Belgium and Sweden.[10]

A crisis, possibly on the scale of the 'revisionism' debate, threatened the unity of the party. It was up to Kautsky and Bebel to reach a compromise. Opposing the position of the trade unions and the right wing, who called for a refutation of the entire concept of a mass strike, they hesitantly supported Luxemburg's contention that the mass strike be included in the social democratic arsenal – but only as a defensive tactic.

The response in the bourgeois press was hysterical. Luxemburg was castigated as an anti-German Jew, a bloodthirsty woman, and a hypocrite. The Reverend Friedrich Naumann, a leader of the 'liberal' Progressive Party, attacked her personally for supporting the bloodshed in the east while sitting safely in Germany.[11]

Stung by the challenge, Rosa Luxemburg – under the pseudonym Anna Matschke – left immediately for Warsaw, then still part of the Russian Empire, where revolution was also in progress. There she experienced first-hand the power and innovative possibilities of the masses themselves in democratically organising themselves and establishing discipline. This is conveyed vividly in one of her letters of the time:

> a quiet heroism and a feeling of solidarity are developing among the masses which I would very much like to show to the dear Germans. Workers everywhere are, by themselves, reaching agreements whereby, for instance, the employed give up one day's wages every week for the unemployed. Or, where employment is reduced to four days a week, there they arrange it in such a way that no one is laid off, but that everyone works a few hours less per week. All this is done as a matter of course, with such simplicity and smoothness that the Party is informed of it only in passing. In fact, the feeling of solidarity and brotherhood is so strongly developed that you can't help but be amazed even though you have personally worked for its development. And then too, an interesting result of the revolution: in all factories, committees have arisen 'on their own', elected by the workers, which decide on all matters relating to

working conditions, hirings and firings of workers, etc. The employer has actually ceased being 'the master in his own house'. A curious little example: recently the management of a factory wanted to punish several workers for being very late. The factory committee prevented this: whereupon the factory owner lodged a complaint with the Committee of the Social Democratic Party, claiming that the factory committee was 'not acting in accordance with social democratic principles' since the Social Democratic Party stands for diligent and honest fulfilment of obligations! And so in one case after the other.[12]

By 1906, the Tsarist police had arrested her. But, the Warsaw experience was formative since it showed Luxemburg what could happen when a working class manifested its 'sovereignty'. Despite the fact that she did not grasp the centrality of the proletariat's new organisational form, *the soviet*, she did observe that democracy was being extended beyond the bounds of bourgeois liberalism. Indeed, from this experience, it became clear to her that democracy held a potential beyond the circumscribed equality of rights of the bourgeois democratic state. Though the importance of these rights could not be ignored, Luxemburg realised that democracy could never be fulfilled under the material exploitation of the capitalist system. Even these rights themselves could not be fully utilised while material exploitation continued and, therefore, the exploitative system and the bourgeoisie itself would have to be suppressed. But this could only be done through the dictatorship of a class which would *extend* democracy from the political into the socio-economic realm.

It is this type of self-contained proletarian *sovereignty* which underlies Luxemburg's theory of the mass strike along with the relation between party and mass. The mass strike for Luxemburg was neither the apex of revolution, as it was for the anarchists, nor a 'myth' in the Sorelian sense. Rather, it was a stage within the revolutionary conflict itself. During that stage, the artificial division between political and economic organisation would start to be overcome and the working class could begin the manifold social experiment of organising itself in new ways.

7. The Revolutions in Russia: Democracy and Mass Strike

'Mass Strike, Party and Trade Unions' is perhaps Luxemburg's most important theoretical work. Like all Second International social democrats, Luxemburg feared 'putschism'. But, unlike most of these same social democrats, she also feared the power and hubris of the party apparatus. On the one hand she claimed that 'I envisage neither a sudden "descent into the street" nor some haphazard adventure',[1] on the other she criticised the growth of 'parliamentary cretinism'.

The mass strike was the means whereby the proletariat would avoid falling into either of these organisational errors. In the mass strike, the 'latent' political consciousness of the working class – which cannot receive expression through parliamentary activity or 'economistic' trade union struggles – becomes 'active'. But, it does so only when two conditions are met: when the economic and political struggles are unified and when the party itself assumes its pedagogical relationship with the masses.

The first condition confronted the widely accepted 'twin pillar' theory of social democratic action whereby the trade unions were considered to be the economic arm and the party the political arm of the labour movement.[2] In Luxemburg's view, mounting calls for trade union independence would necessarily hurt party unity and also split issues off from one another thereby hindering class consciousness regarding the 'totality' to be transformed. Still, it is important to note that

> the progress of the movement on the whole is not expressed in the fact that the initial economic stage is left out, but rather in the rapidity with which all the stages to the political demonstration are run through, and in the extremity of the point to which the strike moves forward.[3]

Precisely because the true revolutionary content of social democracy lay in its political demands, and because the possibility of revolutionary action was predicated upon the translation of economic into political class consciousness, Rosa Luxemburg would call for a reorientation of social democratic theory with regard to the impending struggle. She wrote:

> In a revolutionary mass action the political and economic struggles are one, and the artificial barriers between the unions and social democracy which make them two separate, totally independent forms of the labour movement will simply be washed away. But, what finds concrete expression in the revolutionary mass movement is also the case for the parliamentary period. There are not two different class struggles of the working class, an economic and a social one. Rather, there is only *one* class struggle which is directed at the same time at the limitation of capitalistic exploitation within the bourgeois society and at the abolition of exploitation together with bourgeois society.[4]

It is this bifurcation of the struggle, resulting in a subordination of the political, which still haunts contemporary socialism. This cannot, however, be remedied by having the party simply 'call' a mass strike. Luxemburg always recognised that it is impossible to 'make' a revolution by decree at any point in time and that the objective circumstances which radicalise the masses must be extant.[5] In her debates with Bernstein and then Kautsky, she also made clear that revolutionary action can always be considered 'premature' since it is always possible to claim that objective conditions are not 'ripe' enough.

Consequently, Luxemburg wished to avoid both voluntarism and objectivism in her conception of the mass strike. In order to overcome both of these pitfalls, she argued for *preparatory work* by the party to build the consciousness of the working class; such work calls upon the party to analyse the current situation in a coherent revolutionary manner and develop the revolutionary tactics for it. This is not simply a technical matter for the organisation. Rather, it involves the party in a commitment to the *process* wherein the consciousness of the masses can be pedagogically raised. Thus:

> Instead of puzzling its head with the technical side, with the mechanism of the mass strike, social democracy is called to take over the *political* leadership, even in the midst of the revolutionary period. To give slogans, the direction of the struggle; to organise the *tactics* of the political struggle in such a way that in every phase and in every moment of the struggle the whole sum of the available and already released active power of the proletariat will be realised and find expression in the battle stance of the party; to see that the resoluteness and acuteness of the tactics of social democracy never fall *below* the level of the actual relation of forces but rather rise above it – that is the most important task of the 'leadership' in the period of the mass strike.[6]

Based upon her belief in the need *to build* 'friction' between classes, Luxemburg conceives of the mass strike as a process. In her view it is completely absurd to think of the mass strike as an isolated action. The 'mass strike is rather the sign, the totality-concept of a whole period of the class struggle lasting for years, perhaps decades'.[7] And, as a process, as 'the phenomenal form of the proletarian struggle in revolution',[8] the mass strike, cannot be conceived either as a purely 'defensive' tactic or as subordinate to parliamentarism. No revolution can be made according to some abstract plan. The masses themselves must test their capabilities in the struggle itself. As a product and a producer of revolutionary consciousness, the mass strike is always to some extent experimental. It forms new institutions and then, at a different stage of the struggle, still newer ones.

Luxemburg understood that it was necessary to set a socio-political context such that the possibilities for further activity would be ensured. For this reason, it is not inconsistent that Luxemburg's hopes for the 1905 revolution in Tsarist Russia could be condensed into one word: *republic*. The creation of a republic would make the Russian bourgeoisie accept the power that its counterpart did not accept in Germany in 1848. In other words, it would force the Russian bourgeoisie to remain loyal to

60

the European revolutionary demands of 1789 which would help create the preconditions for a deepening of proletarian class consciousness. Given the growth in working class consciousness through the mass strike, Rosa Luxemburg saw the exacerbation of fundamental class contradictions which would only be aided through the greater possibilities for propaganda and organisation that a republic would provide.

In the same way that her theory of the mass strike opened up a new notion of the relation between party and mass, it called into question the notion of 'success'. The reformist notion of success in terms of small victories was no less repugnant to her than the victory of a Blanquist putsch. Instead, Luxemburg perceived that what was originally a 'success' might well turn into an ultimate failure[9] and, by the same token, what immediately appeared as a failure could create the preconditions for a future success. Thus Luxemburg's emphasis upon the mass strike can also be translated into the demand for a self-conscious retention and elaboration of a revolutionary tradition with an emancipatory goal by the working class.

The apparent 'failure' of the revolution, therefore, did not dampen Luxemburg's belief in the mass strike: not only did it ultimately become a link to 1917; but it also brought about an eight hour working day for a brief period, forced a Duma (parliament) into existence, and exposed the weakness of the bourgeoisie in the Duma that was set up. Indeed, it became clear to her that 'the manifold Russian bourgeoisie is not able either to protect the given order from ruin or create a new up-to-date legal or political order'.[10] Rather than retreat in the wake of the ensuing counter-revolution, Luxemburg radicalised her views. In a letter to the Latvian social democrats in 1908, she took a position that was close to Lenin's:

> And so, after three years of the most difficult attempts, we find ourselves faced once again with the Gordian knot: neither the liberal bourgeoisie nor its artificial unification with the revolutionary proletariat can actualise the task of the Russian revolution. Only the independent activity of the proletariat as a class, supported by the revolutionary movement of the peasants, will be able to destroy

61

absolutism and introduce political freedom into Russia. This is the most irrefutable and most important lesson from the history of revolutionary development.[11]

Unfortunately Rosa Luxemburg's European comrades did not agree. Instead, the increasing bureaucratic petrification, the new chauvinism and the Kautskyan 'strategy of attrition'[12] led to her defeat in the mass strike debate in 1910 and, perhaps more importantly, to her complete isolation on the Polish question.

The position that she put forward in 1908 was precisely the one that would inform her analysis through the revolution of 1917. From 1905 to 1917, there is no break in her values or modes of evaluation: what she learned in the 1905 'dress rehearsal' was to guide her when the curtain went up for the great historical drama initiated by the Bolsheviks.

Her analysis of the events in October of 1917, 'The Russian Revolution' was not published in her lifetime for fear of giving support to the counter-revolution. Yet, certain critics continue to employ it as a blanket condemnation of the Bolsheviks. It is nothing of the kind. Luxemburg's critique is clearly directed from the *left*.[13] Indeed, she viewed the Russian Revolution as the potential 'salvation' of Europe and the opening of a new epoch in world history. Following upon her insight of 1905 that the centre of revolutionary gravity had shifted from Europe to Russia, she hoped that the Russian events would spark the European working class. In fact, support from the western proletariat became the crucial assumption which all major figures of the Revolution shared.

Written in prison, amidst the collapse of the German war effort, Luxemburg's analysis of Russian events is as trenchant and farsighted as any that has been made of a world historical event. It begins with a critique of the Bolshevik agrarian policy. It is true that the Bolsheviks would have had enormous trouble capturing the loyalty of the peasantry had they not put forward the slogan: 'Go and take the land for yourselves!' But, in contrast to many, Luxemburg immediately saw the dangerous implications of this policy for the *future* of the revolution. She realised that inequality among the peasants would *increase* and that class antagonisms within the peasantry would be sharpened so that 'a new and

62

powerful layer of popular enemies of socialism in the countryside [will arise], enemies whose resistance will be much more dangerous and stubborn than that of the large landowners and the nobility.'[14] She saw that this new stratum of property owning peasants, because their interests were fundamentally opposed to any socialisation of the economy, would come into conflict with the industrial working class itself. The result could only be a conflict between 'town and country'.[15] And Luxemburg was proved right. The policy of the Bolsheviks did indeed lead to the agrarian problem of the late twenties and thirties – a problem for which Stalin had his own grisly solution.

There was also the old controversy over the 'right of self-determination'. For Luxemburg, this 'hollow, nationalist phraseology' should not have been injected into the revolutionary struggle at all.[16] From her standpoint, the inclusion of this slogan could only cause the greatest confusion for the international proletariat. By not 'working for the most compact union of the revolutionary forces throughout the area of the empire', by not 'defending tooth and nail the integrity of the Russian Empire as an area of revolution and opposing all forms of separatism, the solidarity and inseparability of the proletarians of all lands within the sphere of the Russian Revolution',[17] Lenin and the Bolsheviks found themselves in a quagmire. They were eventually forced into the position of offering independence to nations over which the Bolsheviks had no control and denying it to those over which their control was manifest. In short, Luxemburg was right once again; Lenin's assumption that Bolshevik support for the national movements in the Russian border states would create faithful allies for the revolution proved false.[18]

Most important is her criticism of the Bolshevik decision to dissolve the Constituent Assembly. Much has been written about the dire straits in which the Bolsheviks found themselves after the revolution, straits which would justify the abolition of an Assembly in which they were the minority. Faced with a ravaged countryside, invasion, civil war and economic isolation, many claim that the step had to be taken. Indeed, Luxemburg herself realised that the old Constituent Assembly – 'which reflected the Kerenskyan Russia of yesterday, of the period of vacillations and coalition with the bourgeoisie'[19] – should have been abolished. From Luxemburg's standpoint, however, a new constituent assembly should have been convened.

The difference here does not merely involve a matter of tactics, but a fundamentally different conception of revolution itself. In Luxemburg's view the curtailment of democracy becomes a cure that is worse than the disease. Dissolution of the Constituent Assembly necessarily curtailed the initiative of the masses – the only corrective to bureaucratic degeneration.

> Public control is indispensably necessary. Otherwise the exchange of experience is only possible within the closed circle of the new regime. Corruption becomes inevitable. Socialism in life demands a complete spiritual transformation in the masses degraded by centuries of bourgeois class rule. Social instincts in place of egoistical ones, mass initiatives in place of inertia, idealism which conquers all suffering, etc. No one knows this better than Lenin. But he is completely mistaken in the means he employs. Decree, dictatorial force of the factory overseer, Draconian penalties, rule by terror – all these things are but palliatives. The only way to a rebirth is the school of public life itself, the most unlimited, the broadest democracy and public opinion. It is the rule by terror which demoralises . . . Only experience is capable of correcting and opening new ways. Only unobstructed, effervescing life falls into a thousand new forms and improvisations, brings to light creative forces itself, corrects all mistaken attempts. The public life of countries with limited freedom is so poverty-stricken, so miserable, so rigid, so unfruitful, precisely because through the exclusion of democracy, it cuts off the living sources of all spiritual riches and progress. (Proof: the year 1905 and the months from February to October 1917). There it was political in character; the same thing applies to economic and social life also. The whole mass of the people must take part in it. Otherwise, socialism will be decreed from behind a few official desks by a dozen intellectuals.[20]

Even if the closing of the Assembly could be justified as revolutionary within the Russian context, its effect upon the international socialist community was detrimental. At this point, albeit unintentionally, a contradiction begins to assert itself between national revolutionary needs and the possibilities for international solidarity within the socialist movement. For the Russian Revolution had originally been greeted with tremendous acclaim and even received support from significant sections of the old social democratic movement. Abolishing the Constituent Assembly, however, created a breach between social democrats and communists. This act essentially denied the possibility of a viable socialist opposition and began the centralisation of power that would result in the death of pluralism. Thus, a flood of criticism fell upon the Soviet Union and isolated its supporters in the west from the bulk of the working class which had consistently fought for democracy under the tutelage of the Second International.

Luxemburg recognised that the potential relations of power between a representative government and the soviets could not be determined *a priori*.[21] If the primacy of the soviets could have been guaranteed then support for the Constituent Assembly might be dismissed as petty bourgeois parliamentarism. Indeed, under the stress of the Spartacus uprising, Rosa Luxemburg admitted that she had made a tactical mistake in supporting the Russian Constituent Assembly.[22] Nonetheless, her work unfolds the real dynamic that was in operation; it was a dynamic which would result in the elimination of the soviets along with the Assembly. And they would disappear because:

> with the repression of political life in the land as a whole, life in the soviets must also become more and more crippled. Without general elections, without unrestricted freedom of press and assembly, without a free struggle of opinion, life dies out in every public institution, becomes a mere semblance of life, in which only the bureaucracy remains as the active element. Public life gradually falls asleep, a few dozen party leaders of inexhaustible energy and boundless experience direct and rule. Among them, in reality only a dozen outstanding heads do the leading and an elite of the working class is invited from time to time to meetings where they are to applaud the speeches of the leaders, and to approve proposed resolutions unanimously

65

– at bottom, then, a clique affair – a dictatorship, to be sure, not the dictatorship of the proletariat, however, but only the dictatorship of a handful of politicians, that is a dictatorship in the bourgeois sense, in the sense of the rule of the Jacobins.[23]

For Luxemburg, the choice is not between bourgeois democracy or dictatorship. She opposed both Kautsky and Lenin by claiming that while it is wrong to renounce the socialist revolution due to its 'premature' nature and thus become a devotee of bourgeois democratic forms, it is also a mistake to eliminate democracy in the name of the dictatorship of the proletariat.[24]

In contrast, she developed her conception of the proletarian dictatorship in the following way:

> This dictatorship consists in the *manner of applying democracy*, not in its elimination, in energetic, resolute attacks upon the well-entrenched rights and economic relationships of bourgeois society, without which a socialist transformation cannot be accomplished. But this dictatorship must be the work of the *class* and not of a little leading minority in the name of the class – that is, it must proceed step by step out of the active participation of the masses; it must be under their direct influence, subjected to the control of complete public activity; it must arise out of the growing political training of the mass of the people.[25]

In contrast to so many liberal critics of the Revolution, Luxemburg always understood events in Russia within an international context. She also understood fully that the disastrous conditions in which the Russian Revolution took place would necessarily 'distort' any socialist policy and that, if the revolution failed in Russia, it would in large part be due to the inability of the European working class to carry out its own revolution to support the industrially backward Russians. Thus, in a telling letter to Adolf Warski in 1918, she wrote of the terror:

> To be sure, terrorism indicates fundamental weakness, but the terror is directed against internal enemies whose hopes rest upon the continuation of capitalism outside Russia

66

and who receive support and encouragement for their views from abroad. If the European revolution takes place, the Russian counter-revolutionaries will not only lose this support, but – more importantly – their courage as well. In short, the terror in Russia is above all an expression of the weakness of the European proletariat.[26]

Once again, Luxemburg's internationalism comes to the fore. Add to this her romantic view of socialist democracy and her sense of the revolution as a process and it is possible to predict what she will see as 'essential' in the Bolshevik experience. Ultimately:

It is not a matter of this or that secondary question of tactics, but of the capacity of the proletariat for action, the strength to act, the will to power of socialism as such. In this Lenin, Trotsky and their friends were the *first*, those who went ahead as an example to the proletariat of the world; they are still the *only ones* up to now who can cry with Hutten: 'I have dared!'

This is the essential and *enduring* in Bolshevik policy. In *this* sense, theirs is the immortal historical service of having marched at the head of the international proletariat with the conquest of political power and the practical placing of the problem of the realisation of socialism, and of having advanced mightily the settlement of the score between capital and labour in the entire world. In Russia the problem could only be posed. It could not be solved in Russia. And in *this* sense, the future everywhere belongs to 'Bolshevism.'[27]

8. Correspondence: Friends and Lovers

To regard Rosa Luxemburg's circle as just another clique in an international socialist movement, which was notorious for the cliques it engendered, is to miss the point. Although she became acquainted in her youth with subsequent leaders of the SDKPL and the Bolshevik movement – such as Leo Jogiches, Julek Marchlewski, Feliks Dzerzinski, and Adolf Warski – in the larger world of German social democracy and the Second International her close friends were anything but powerful. Almost self-consciously, Luxemburg always preserved a certain distance from Bebel, Liebknecht, and even Kautsky. Thus, her immediate circle was not one that could protect her from the machinations of other cliques within the movement.

One of the most striking features of Luxemburg's correspondence is that it shows how very narrow was her circle of intimates. And this was not simply a matter of choice. Though practically every comrade who ever met Luxemburg remembered her as 'Rosa', she was a difficult and temperamental person. Few friendships remained constant through her lifetime, and it is clear that not more than a handful ever grew close to her.

She was often arbitrary in choosing both her friends and her enemies. She respected opponents like Lenin, Jaures and, to a certain extent, even Bernstein. She also thought highly of Alexander Helphand (Parvus) who was decisive in formulating the concept of the 'permanent revolution' and who became a major force on the international left before he turned to German chauvinism. Yet, she detested the good-natured Kantian socialist Kurt Eisner, later the Prime Minister of the ill-fated Bavarian Soviet Republic. Also she despised Trotsky and the cynical Karl Radek who was one of her most gifted students and who would play a major role in the founding of the German Communist Party (KPD), as well as in the Third International, the Trotskyist opposition and Stalin's foreign service until his death in the purges.

Thus politics was only one element of friendship. Though Rosa Luxemburg's letters are all written to socialists, many of her friends were basically apolitical people who involved themselves with politics fundamentally out of loyalty to her. Gertrud Zlottko, Hans Diefenbach, and Mathilde Jacob, who ran such heavy risks smuggling Luxemburg's letters and manuscripts out of prison,[1] fall into this category and their actions become a testament to the loyalty that Rosa Luxemburg inspired.

Another point becomes important in this context. In contrast to the brilliant group of Polish organisers and intellectuals whom she knew in Zurich, the friends she chose when she entered the German scene were anything but her intellectual equals. Once again, Kautsky was to a certain extent the exception. Yet, even in her letters to him – and especially in her correspondence with Luise Kautsky, Mathilde Jacob, Sonja Liebknecht, and Hans Diefenbach – there is little resemblance to Marx's remarkable correspondence with his contemporaries or to the fascinating letters that were exchanged between Bebel, Kautsky, and Victor Adler, the leader of the Austrian Social Democratic Party. Luxemburg did not generally argue over matters of theory or history with her close friends. In the intellectual realm, she was fully aware of her superiority. In fact, what was probably most important to Luxemburg in the friends that she chose was a lack of pretentiousness, a warmth, and even a certain naivety. The members of her little group helped to create a secure private realm that stood beyond the political sphere. It was this circle which gave Rosa the opportunity to express her inner needs and feelings with an effusiveness that stands in sharp contrast to the formal role she had to play in politics and to the caution that she had to exhibit in public.

Her private world was always essential to Rosa Luxemburg. Again and again, she maintained that she was happier sitting in a garden than at a party congress. Over and over, in her letters to Jogiches, she demanded a stable home life. Indeed, after her death, friends like Henriette Roland-Holst and Luise Kautsky sought to show that Rosa Luxemburg was fundamentally an apolitical person.[2] But, as J. P. Nettl, one of her biographers, correctly states: 'the idea of having to choose between the woman of the red revolution and the woman of the pink window-boxes is ludicrous and arbitrary'.[3] There can be little question that Rosa Luxemburg demanded both a secure private life and an active political one – and clearly one served to balance the other.

The security that Rosa Luxemburg was able to find in her circle was to some extent based upon the tyranny that she was able to exert. When disagreements arose, she would brook no opposition. Taking all her close friends into account, there was only one person who could consistently stand up to her: Leo Jogiches, her first great love. A man of action about whom still not enough is known, Jogiches always preferred to remain in the background. Secretive and furtive to the point of paranoia, Jogiches was the organisational power behind the SKDPL and later the Spartacus League. His egoism was legendary and yet Jogiches was a completely dedicated socialist who used his considerable fortune for the movement without any thought of personal gain.

For the most part, the correspondence between them expresses the conflict for primacy in both the personal and political arenas. Again and again, Luxemburg consciously seeks to convince Jogiches of her independence and also to force him to acknowledge her success within the most prestigious organisation in the socialist world. In these letters, the strength of the woman, and her extraordinary sense of honour and daring, sparkle on every page. But these letters are not simply concerned with the personal; Luxemburg discusses her own political decisions and party affairs as well. The political views of Luxemburg and Jogiches were intertwined from the very first, and she always asked his detailed advice on political questions – particularly in the early years. Their emotional intimacy ended when Jogiches had an affair with another comrade while he was underground. Nevertheless, their working relationship continued until her death and it was Jogiches who, although once again underground and with his life in constant danger following the Spartacus insurrection, led the press investigation into the circumstances of her murder.

Another close friend of Rosa's was Clara Zetkin. Rosa Luxemburg had known her since the Stuttgart Congress in 1898,

70

and though Luxemburg had little interest in the women's movement and its magazine *Die Gleichheit* ('Equality') of which Zetkin was the editor, they became lifelong friends. The relationship is particularly interesting since Luxemburg always viewed class – and by this she meant the concept derived from the actual process of production – as central; in the same way that working class consciousness was to transcend national and racial differences, so was it to transcend sexual ones as well. In short, Rosa Luxemburg refused to place her own subjective experience of being a woman – or being a Jew – beyond the fundamental objective contradiction within capitalist society: the contradiction between social production and private appropriation. But, this is not to say that the oppression of women, Jews, or other groups should be ignored. Her position was very clear:

> The proposition that Social Democracy is the representative of the class interests of the proletariat but that it is at the same time the representative of all the progressive interests of society and of all oppressed victims of bourgeois society is not to be understood as saying that in the program of Social Democracy all these interests are ideally synthesized. This proposition becomes true through the process of historical development by which Social Democracy, as a political party, gradually becomes the haven of the different dissatisfied elements of society, becoming a party of the people opposed to a tiny minority of capitalist rulers. But Social Democracy must always know how to subordinate the present pains of this colorful herd of recruits to the ultimate goals of the working class; it must know how to integrate the non-proletarian spirit of opposition into revolutionary proletarian action; in a word, it must know how to assimilate, to digest these elements which come to it.[4]

As against followers of the bourgeois women's movement, or feminists of the party right like Lili Braun, for Rosa Luxemburg it would have made as little sense to speak of the real emancipation of women in capitalist society as it would have for Marx to speak of the emancipation of the Jews. In this regard, Rosa Luxemburg and Clara Zetkin were not as far apart as it might initially seem. Although Luxemburg clearly evidenced less interest in women's issues than Zetkin, even for the latter any discussion of liberating women without working class action would have been unthinkable.

In general Clara Zetkin took a back seat to her friend on intellectual and political matters. She objected strongly, however, to Luxemburg's brief affair with her younger son. Luxemburg saw Zetkin's stance as a prime example of hypocrisy. For his part, Kostia Zetkin felt pressure from both sides and so the affair ended quickly. It was after her break with Kostia that Rosa Luxemburg formed her last attachment: to Hans Diefenbach.

Neither Kostia Zetkin nor Hans Diefenbach had the personal magnetism of Jogiches. Both bowed to her will. Particularly in the case of Diefenbach, whom Rosa Luxemburg quite consciously sought to take in hand, the contrast with Jogiches is striking. Yet, Rosa loved him dearly. After his death in 1917 she was overcome with grief. Her letters to him reveal a lack of self-consciousness, an openness and humanity that are missing in her correspondence with Jogiches. They also clearly show her desire that he become decisive, that he exert himself intellectually and that he develop his personal potential to the utmost.

This was also the case with her female friends. After her relationship with Jogiches, Luxemburg often urged the women in her circle to take a personal stand for independence – particularly when their spouses had become political enemies, as in the cases of Luise Kautsky and Mathilde Wurm. She sought to develop the character of her close friends by forcing them to reflect upon the various influences to which they were subject and make their own choices.

Indeed, what truly marks her correspondence is the most fundamental value of her revered Goethe: 'personality'. Probably it was this quality of Rosa Luxemburg's which created such an extraordinary loyalty to her on the part of her friends, and nowhere does it become clearer than in her remarkable *Letters from Prison*. Particularly in prison, her letters assume a lyrical power of poetic proportions as her gaze shifts from the infighting within the International to the little world of her confinement: a world of insects, plants, and birds.

Rosa Luxemburg was incarcerated for most of the First World War, and this period was the most difficult of her life. By the time of her release in 1918, she was visibly altered; she had withered and her hair had turned completely white. While in prison, she suffered terribly from stomach problems and from her nerves. Still, Luxemburg remained intellectually active; there was the Korolenko translation as well as a few remarkable brochures such as the *Anti-Critique* and the *Junius Pamphlet*. She read voluminously: geology, animal husbandry, literary criticism, political economy, plays, biographies, history, and more. In the daytime, she took her short walks and searched for beauty in the cracks of existence; as a response to the boredom of her imprisonment, she watched insects, fed her titmice and observed the manifold diversity of nature. At night, she recited passages from Shakespeare, Goethe, and Mörike to relieve her loneliness.

The picture of Rosa Luxemburg in prison is that of a Renaissance woman; the anti-intellectualism of the pseudo-radical and an escape into nature no less than the *apparatchik* mentality of Stalinism are foreign to her. Indeed, the popular image of the revolutionary as a dour, sneering, paranoid automaton bears little resemblance to this spirited woman trying to construct a semblance of life in her tiny cell.

The world somehow remains open to her and her letters bristle with a vitality and lyricism that allowed Rosa Luxemburg to affirm her sense of self and her spontaneity which was always in danger of being liquidated. She overcame any temptation to be self-indulgent, for she knew that many of her friends – particularly Sonja Liebknecht whose husband was also incarcerated – were susceptible to personal depression and political despair. Especially in the letters written to Sonja Liebknecht, Rosa sought to dispel this depression by shifting Sonja's focus from the horror of the immediate political reality to the occasional moments of beauty and happiness that could still be found in its midst.

Not that Rosa Luxemburg wanted to escape the political realm. The possibility of change always exists on the horizon; the objective contradictions of capitalist society do not disappear and the individual must stay on the alert to any emerging crisis. It is important to make the lyrical moment of politics clear, and this is precisely what Rosa Luxemburg does when she writes:

> The psyche of the masses, like the eternal sea always carries all the latent possibilities: the deathly calm and the roaring storm, the lowest cowardice and the wildest heroism. The mass is always that which it *must* be according to the circumstances of the time, and the mass is always at the point of becoming something different than what it appears to be.[5]

This letter reflects the romanticism, the revolutionary hope and the militancy, which Rosa Luxemburg's friends and followers associated with her name. But, particularly during the Spartacus revolt, she was pilloried by opponents within the SPD and without. 'Bloody Rosa!', 'The Female Terror!', 'Murderer!', 'Nihilist!' – such was the bloodthirsty image which her name conjured in the minds of the populace. But, then, a particular letter – which was included in the *Letters from Prison* – caused a scandal for her opponents and stimulated a new popular evaluation which exposed Luxemburg's kindness, sensitivity, and humanity. Strangely enough, it was about a buffalo:

> A few days ago, a wagon loaded with sacks drove into the prison. The cargo was piled up so high that the buffaloes could not make it over the threshold of the gateway. The attending soldier, a brutal character, began to beat away at the animals with the heavy end of his whip so savagely that the overseer indignantly called him to account. 'Don't you have any pity for the animals?' 'No one has any pity for us people either!' he answered with an evil laugh and fell upon them ever more forcefully . . . Finally, the animals started up and got over the hump, but one of them was bleeding . . . Sonitschka, buffalo hide is proverbial for its thickness and toughness, and it was lacerated. Then, during the unloading, the animals stood completely still, exhausted, and one, the one that was bleeding, all the while looked ahead with an expression on its black face and in its soft black eyes like that of a weeping child who has been severely punished and who does not know why, what for, who does not know how to escape the torment and the

74

brutality . . . I stood facing the animal and it looked at me; tears were running from my eyes – they were *his* tears. One cannot quiver any more painfully over one's dearest brother's sorrow than I quivered in my impotence over this silent anguish.

How far, how irretrievably lost, are the free, succulent, green pastures of Rumania! How different it was with the sun shining, the wind flowing; how different were the beautiful sounds of birds, the melodious calls of shepherds. And here: this strange weird city, the fusty stable, the nauseating mouldy hay mixed with putrid straw, the strange, horrible people – and the blows, the blood running from the fresh wound . . . Oh! My poor buffalo! My poor beloved brother! We both stand here so powerless and spiritless and are united only in pain, in powerlessness and in longing . . .

Meanwhile, the prisoners bustled busily about the wagon, unloading the heavy sacks and carrying them into the building. The soldier, however, stuck both hands into his pockets, strolled across the yard with great strides, smiled and softly whistled a popular song. And the whole glorious war passed in front of my eyes.[6]

She ends that long letter with the injunction to remain 'calm and cheerful' in spite of everything. As graphically as Luxemburg can convey the image of horror, so can she inspire the will to revolt, the will to keep struggling for a happier and more humane order. In this sense, Rosa Luxemburg comes to incarnate what the philosopher Ernst Bloch has called 'militant optimism'. This optimism does not simply involve the passive belief that 'everything will turn out all right', or a belief in fate, or even an unquestioning belief in the objective 'historical' laws of the dialectic. Instead, it calls for a consistent engagement in order to *make* everything turn out all right through struggle.

Rosa Luxemburg does not simply dismiss the personal demand for happiness in the name of this struggle. Her revolt is not only political, but personal as well. A militant hope for social change merges with a personal demand – the demand for a measure of happiness in the face of the most brutal oppression.

In prison, the literature that was so dear to her partially helped meet this demand. But, more generally, in contrast to the cynical pessimism and despair that has followed the 1960s, Luxemburg's sense of 'militant optimism' sets us an example. It is in this way that Rosa Luxemburg's life assumes a relevance and value for those of us on the left.

9. The Socialist Left – On the Defensive

By 1910, the SPD was far different from what it was at the time when Rosa Luxemburg had first called upon the party to reaffirm its principles in the face of the revisionist threat. What was once a rag-tag party had become an organisation. The party's

> assets ran into millions and it controlled a huge number of subsidiary organisations. It owned vast newspapers and publishing houses and great printing works. It had innumerable offices and halls and was often involved in administering and building societies and both consumers' and producers' co-operatives. A staff of thousands of secretaries, editors, employees, workers and officials was required to operate this huge Labour movement and administer its manifold enterprises.[1]

Under the pressure of electoral campaigns, trade union activity and the image of a responsible 'national' party, an integration into the prevailing order had taken place. Whether the reactionary elements of the German Empire recognised the fact or not, the values of imperialism, nationalism and German *Kultur* were creeping forward in the SPD through a new breed: the party hack. This breed had not gone through the party's formative years. But, aided by those who had made their peace with absolutism after the Anti-Socialist laws were lifted, they infused the SPD with a new sense of 'compromise' and 'pragmatism'.

Rosa Luxemburg witnessed the developing petrification within the party with horror and, ever more vehemently, reiterated a position which she had implicitly outlined in 1898. At the point where marxist theory was becoming completely divorced from reformist praxis, Luxemburg consistently argued against what was known as the 'two-stage' theory of revolution

77

by emphasising that there are not two rigidly demarcated phases of the proletarian struggle: capitalism and the transition to socialism. The fusion of these two phases, however, would only be possible once the party had committed itself to build up the consciousness of the working class for its 'decisive clash' with the bourgeoisie.[2]

Of course, Luxemburg did not disregard electoral activity, or demands for suffrage and civil liberties. But, she was adamant that they should not become ends in themselves. For Luxemburg, all such demands assume their importance only insofar as they create the context in which a more radical development of working class politics and consciousness can arise.[3] Thus, in her view, the formal liberties of bourgeois democracy become the *sine qua non* for revolutionary action which will extend them into the socio-economic life of the working class.

This is why Luxemburg supported political reform in some circumstances as well as the mass strike when there was a potential for more radical action. Always at stake was the heightening of the 'proletarian public sphere',[4] which was endangered by the bureaucratic ossification of the party.

It was for this reason that Rosa Luxemburg began to address her appeals over the heads of the party leadership to the masses themselves. This is what made access to the press so important. For it must be remembered that the SPD – like the Second International – retained a democratic dimension. The party hierarchy was somewhat checked by its press, where radicals often held control, and the Reichstag delegation could often exert a countervailing influence on the bureaucracy until at least a decade into the twentieth century.[5] Although bureaucratic petrification was under way, a broad variety of viewpoints could be represented and heard within the socialist camp during most of Bebel's ascendancy.

The existence of radicals within the party was not merely for show. They exerted an influence that went far beyond the size of their group. Parvus and Julek Marchlewski – radicals and foreigners who had been expelled by the royal government of Saxony – could push through Rosa Luxemburg's appointment as editor of the *Sächsische Arbeiter-Zeitung*; at the *Leipziger Volkszeitung*, Franz Mehring arranged for her appointment as co-editor after Bruno Schönlank's death; she was also a contributing editor to *Die Neue Zeit*.

As the rigidity of the party bureaucracy increased, the possibility of access to the press became ever more critical for Rosa Luxemburg. Indeed, the years following the Bernstein debate were marked by an extraordinary output and ceaseless political activity. It is fair to say, that by 1905 Rosa Luxemburg had reached the peak of her influence within the SPD and was widely acclaimed as the principle representative for the left wing of the International.

Yet, the very year that highlighted the influence of the left – due to the revolutionary events in Russia – also marked the start of a decline which resulted in her ever-increasing isolation within the international socialist movement. Where Luxemburg viewed the Russian mass strike and the self-organisation of the working class as examples to be followed by the German movement, the entrenched bureaucracy and the reformist trade union leaders made their position clear: 'The general strike is general nonsense'.

The right wing of the party was still rejoicing over the 1903 election which had given the SPD its largest electoral victory: 81 seats in the Reichstag and over three million votes.[6] Yet, by 1907, the party was to suffer its most severe defeat. Through an appeal to nationalism, militarism and colonialism, the ultra-conservative von Bülow government scored a resounding victory at the polls by drawing upon that very middle class which Bernstein and the reformists had sought to win over to the socialist cause.

In that same year, the Second International took up the matter of world war. From Algiers and Tunisia to China, the major European powers were involving themselves in one crisis after another. A major conflagration threatened and resolutions were proposed to the Executive of the Second International by Jaurès and Bebel amongst others. The most famous was the one which was overwhelmingly accepted by the convention. This was the resolution proposed by Luxemburg, Lenin, and Martov to strengthen international socialism in its commitment to peace.[7] However, the fundamentally pacifist resolution remained abstract insofar as the International did not have the power to force national parties to comply.

There was not much that could be done when the right-wing of the SPD unleashed its fury in the wake of electoral defeat. As praise for imperialistic ventures dramatically increased, support emerged for strengthening Germany's navy.[8] At the same time, the party executive consolidated itself as a separate bureaucracy. Radicalism within the party was blamed for the electoral setback and the unity of the left wing began to dissolve as Luxemburg grew ever more at odds with Kautsky.

Personal dislike had been building on both sides since the aftermath of the mass strike debate. In 1909 and 1910, an open and bitter split occurred between Rosa Luxemburg and her former patron and friend which had enormous ramifications for the future of German social democracy. The real cause of the split was Kautsky's elaboration of his famous 'strategy of attrition' (*Ermattungsstrategie*). This was a strategy based on the desire to 'defend' existing privileges against the burgeoning rightwing reaction both within the party and in society at large.

Kautsky's position, however, was untenable. On the one hand, he wished to maintain the 'revolutionary phraseology' (Bernstein) and socialist character of the party, while on the other, he wished to placate the fears of reactionary elements in German society. He achieved neither. Where the 'revolutionary phraseology' was simply out of line with the new power of conservatives within the Party, the reactionary strata within the German ruling-class had concerns very different from those of defending the reforms that the SPD had achieved. By neither propagating a radical praxis nor denying his revolutionary posture, the practical consequence of Kautsky's strategy was paralysis. Even more telling was the fact that Kautsky's immobilism came at a time when the conservative reaction in Germany was opposed by the masses themselves. Faced with anti-democratic tendencies, militarist adventures and the loss of reforms, the working class countered with strikes, work stoppages, and demonstrations for suffrage throughout Germany.[9] Thus, to the extent that Kautsky's strategy was directed towards strengthening the commitment to the electoral tactic, it actually involved dampening an emergent revolutionary enthusiasm. Luxemburg viewed this as a basically 'passivist' position and said as much in her article 'What next?'.[10] It was this article that

80

provided the issue for the actual break when Kautsky allegedly interfered with her attempt to publish the piece in *Die Neue Zeit* by editing out her call for a mass strike.[11]

Once the break occurred, Luxemburg attacked with a vengeance. In contrast to Kautsky's 'strategy of attrition', she claimed that existing privileges could only be defended by demanding new ones. For Luxemburg, the moment of political polarisation was precisely the time to re-emphasise the demand for a republic and re-introduce the mass strike as an offensive weapon.[12] Thus, in the face of the rising tide of imperialism, Luxemburg felt that the party had the revolutionary obligation to foster an anti-militarist spirit and intensify the class consciousness of the proletariat no matter what the immediate electoral costs.[13]

The split between Luxemburg and Kautsky led to the division of the radical faction and the formation of three tendencies within the SPD. At one extreme were the reformists like Vollmar, David and Scheidemann, who increasingly advocated support for ruling class imperialist policies. At the other extreme were people like Rosa Luxemburg, Karl Liebknecht, Clara Zetkin and Franz Mehring who were bent on a radical republicanism based on the offensive use of the mass strike. In the middle were the centrists: people like Kautsky, Emanuel Wurm and Alfred Henke, who in theory sought to maintain the traditional policy of the *Erfurt Programme*, but who in practice were moving closer to the right through their support for the 'strategy of attrition'.

The radical left emerged politically weaker than ever and its weakness was only exacerbated by the further bureaucratisation of the party. After Bebel's long illness and death in 1913, this took place under Friedrich Ebert whose name, along with that of Gustav Noske, would come to have a sinister significance for Rosa Luxemburg.

Ebert and Noske typified the party hack. Each had slowly risen through the ranks of the party apparatus; they surveyed the reforms that had been achieved through the growth of the party and sought to build the infrastructure that would guarantee further advances. Bureaucratic and provincial by temperament, they had little use for intellectuals, theoretical debates, or

81

activism on the part of the masses – as Ebert once indicatively remarked: 'I hate the revolution like poison'.

During this period, access to the party press became ever more difficult for the left. Centralisation of power increased after 1912 as the Reichstag membership came under the direct control of the party executive which itself became ever more insulated from the masses though it continued to play upon the old loyalty of party activists. Less and less emphasis was placed upon deepening revolutionary class consciousness and building internationalism within the membership. The result was that when the First World War broke out, a clear majority of the working class favoured entering the fray on chauvinist grounds.

As Luxemburg had foreseen, the reformist petrification of the party went hand in hand with its support for bourgeois nationalist aims. As chauvinism and dreams of imperialist expansion grew in the party, she found herself ever more impotent. But Luxemburg did not simply surrender. As the war approached, she began an assault on party policy that focused on the question of imperialism; it was an assault which would culminate in 1913 with the publication of her major economic work, *The Accumulation of Capital*.

10. Imperialism

Just when Rosa Luxemburg came into open conflict with the guardians of marxist orthodoxy, she began her reassessment of marxist political economy. Beyond the revolutionary phraseology, two schools had arisen regarding the future development of capitalism. On the one hand, there were those who believed that capitalism would produce enough purchasing power to absorb an ever-expanding production of goods; occasionally severe friction might occur, due to the maldistribution of that purchasing power, but no 'breakdown' was inevitable. On the other hand, there were those who felt that production would necessarily outstrip total effective demand due to the technological progress which capitalist social relations would engender; this would lead to a crisis of underconsumption and a 'breakdown' of the system. Basically, the leading followers of Marx in the Second International – Otto Bauer, Bukharin, Hilferding and Lenin – were supporters of the former position whereas Heinrich Cunow and Rosa Luxemburg took the opposing view.

In *The Accumulation of Capital*, Rosa Luxemburg fundamentally sided with the second approach. Given the extraordinary pace of industralisation around the turn of the century, she believed that more goods could be produced cheaper and faster. Following Marx, Luxemburg realised that these goods had to be sold in order for the bourgeoisie to accumulate the capital that would be necessary for the re-investment that would perpetuate the system. In the second volume of *Capital*, however, Marx emphasised the growing imbalance between the increase of these producer goods and the buying power of consumers. But Luxemburg thought Marx had not adequately considered the problems that the latent imbalance between producer and consumer goods would create for the capitalist realisation of profit.

Given this tendency toward over-production of unsale-
able commodities, only two alternatives presented themselves.
Either the capitalist system would immediately collapse due to
a rational unwillingness to invest, or an intermediate alternative
must exist within the very structure of capitalism itself. Such
an alternative would involve the export of those excess goods
into precapitalist territories – in short, imperialism.

Yet, as Marx had already argued, the flow of capitalist
goods into precapitalist areas would itself eventually transform
those primitive societies into industrial ones.[1] Precisely because
capitalism cannot exist as a 'closed' system – that is to say, to the
extent that it must expand into precapitalist areas to ensure its
own survival – the system of capitalism creates its own *historical
limit*.[2] Under present circumstances this historical limit becomes
only *theoretically* apparent. In the meantime it is only possible to
predict recurrent crises, punctuated by military conflicts over
precapitalist markets and resources.[3] But, the economic dynamic
propels capitalism towards its historical limit since the transformation of backward regions will place a boundary on
capitalism's ability to expand so that, ultimately, it will necessarily
implode.[4]

This is the basis of Luxemburg's controversial 'breakdown
theory'. It may even be termed 'objectivist' or 'economistic', not
only because the collapse is inevitable, but also because any real
discussion of the proletariat's role in the process is analytically
neglected. Indeed, as Norman Geras correctly notes, once one
makes the:

> impermissible logical leap which simply equates the
> breakdown of capitalism with the creation of socialism, it is
> mere child's play to construct a completely fatalist and
> allegedly Luxemburgist perspective on the revolutionary
> process. According to this, the laws of capitalist develop-
> ment inevitably issue in economic breakdown and socialist
> revolution, and the consequence and other face of this
> catastrophism is spontaneism, contempt for organisation,
> contempt for leadership and so on. The same inexorable
> economic laws which produce capitalist collapse also
> bring forth mass actions whose spontaneous power and

84

dynamic are sufficient to solve all the political and tactical problems that arise. Taken strictly, this position amounts to the *abolition* of the need for theoretical work, for propaganda and agitation, for organisation and for the preparation for the conquest of political power.[5]

Such reductionist interpretations have been argued often enough.[6] But, the 'impermissible' logic of making the equation between the collapse of capitalism and the rise of socialism becomes evident in the alternative which Luxemburg saw between 'socialism or barbarism'. In each situation, the working class faces a choice which is necessarily related to the *end result* of the process in which it is involved.

It is true that Luxemburg's work is littered with phrases such as 'inevitability' and 'objective necessity'. But, it is precisely here that Luxemburg must be placed within the intellectual tradition from which she emerged. Initially for Hegel, and then more concretely for Marx and even for many of his followers in the Second International, freedom was defined as the understanding of necessity in practice. Thus, the freedom of the working class involved its willingness to act on the contradictory tendencies that capitalism manifested. The hidden presupposition that freedom and necessity are dialectically linked is precisely what results in the *immanent* derivation of the activist moment from the 'objectivist' analysis in *The Accumulation of Capital*. This is why Luxemburg wrote: 'We are the party of class struggle, and not of 'historical laws'.[7]

Once the analysis is put in its historical context political prescriptions arise that fit the socialist vision which Luxemburg elaborated from the very beginning. As against Bernstein or Lenin, Luxemburg was not fundamentally concerned with the particular organisational forms that capital will take, but rather with the systemic conditions that make capitalist accumulation possible in the first place. The essential point of her analysis is that capitalism necessarily *demands* the existence of non-capitalist territories for its own survival. Thus it is logically impossible to oppose capitalism effectively without opposing imperialism as well and, by the same token, the struggle against imperialism can only be waged in terms of the struggle against capitalism.[8]

85

By showing the indissoluble link between capitalism and imperialism, Luxemburg opposes both Lenin's position on self-determination and his later view of imperialism as the 'highest stage' of capitalism. She attempts to demonstrate that, structurally, capitalism is an international system that is intrinsically tied to imperialism and that generates its own limit. In that sense, imperialism is not a 'stage' of capitalism; it merely highlights the capitalist totality in the modern epoch. This argument follows organically from her debate with Bernstein where – despite her recognition of the importance of specific reforms – it becomes essential that the character of capitalism as a total system be made clear to the working class. Because it is intrinsically tied to the capitalist system of production, imperialism cannot be 'reformed' out of existence. From Luxemburg's perspective imperialism cannot be stopped without the abolition of capitalist relations of production. It is true that Luxemburg did not write about the oppositional activity of the colonised in *The Accumulation of Capital*. But she did support the struggle of colonial people in many articles.[9] In her *systemic* analysis, however, it was obviously necessary that she point forward to an international class division,[10] and therefore to the possibility for the transnational unification of the working class – the position that had already been outlined in *The Industrial Development of Poland*.

Once again, for Luxemburg, it is the totality which is to be overcome. Thus, imperialism is not simply the policy of a specific sector of capital, as Hobson believed, or a matter that can be decided case by case, as certain social democrats claimed.

In Luxemburg's view, militarism necessarily accompanies the imperialist development of capitalism and is its domestic manifestation. Already her early controversy with Max Schippel and the right wing of the party foreshadowed this later analysis.[11] Even then, it had already become clear to her that militarism hindered the revolutionary efforts of the working class. Under the impetus of the imperialist dynamic, militarism would become the 'capitalist disease'. Thus, it would set off competing 'national interests' against one another thereby increasingly fostering a chauvinist ideology. It would also provide an ever-present outlet for capital investment. Consequently, militarism would also provide jobs for workers. Any socialist party would therefore be

86

forced into choosing between immediate benefits for the working class and ultimate goals. Choosing the former, however, would naturally elicit the other effect of militarism; it would make the armed forces stronger in that very state which would have to be overthrown.[12]

Because she saw militarism as a moment of imperialism, Rosa Luxemburg found it useless to call for international disarmament conferences.[13] That position clearly no longer makes sense in the nuclear age. Despite her claim that socialism can only exist as an international phenomenon, her argument only partially explains the blatant imperialism of the Soviet Union. The problem is that Luxemburg's position basically denies that imperialism is more a tactic than an imperative for most capitalist states. Nevertheless, particularly in the case of a state which is politically hegemonic, there is a tendency which continues to link capitalism with militarism and imperialism. This will necessarily have a direct impact on militarism throughout the world. In this sense, there is a continuing validity to her claim that the struggle against militarism must be rooted in the international struggle against capitalism.

Of course, there are problems with Luxemburg's analysis. Though she never equated the 'breakdown' of capitalism with the creation of socialism, she did identify it with economic crisis. Unfortunately, the very notion of breakdown remains vague. But however it may be defined, 1929 shows that breakdown is not synonomous with economic crisis *per se*. For 'crisis' is itself a natural phase in the development of capitalism; in Hegelian terms, a crisis is the momentary self-negation of the capitalist economic system wherein accumulation can begin anew. From *Capital* it is possible to glean various tendencies that give rise to crises such as underconsumption, the falling rate of profit, or the decline in size of the industrial reserve army. Any of them may cause a crisis within a given set of socio-historical circumstances; in fact, within the international arena, these phenomena may even appear simultaneously.

But by looking for *one* given cause for crisis – namely underconsumption – Luxemburg boxed herself into an untenable position. This was only exacerbated by the fact that she found only one solution by which capitalism could avert destruction – imperialism. Yet, there are others. Governments can directly or indirectly aid in the accumulation process through subsidies and the development of the welfare state. By the same token, the intensification‾ of exploitation – by material and ideological means – can provide an alternative to implosion. Also monopolies can provide such an alternative by reorganising capital and the accumulation process at the expense of the petty bourgeoisie and the Third World.

Probably, Luxemburg still thought of world development as being spurred by the relatively 'progressive' trusts of 'organised capitalism' (Hilferding). But, the trusts of organised capitalism have given way to the parasitic multinationals of the current era. This is important to the extent that Luxemburg basically envisioned a unified world development in terms of the west. Given the extended range of exploitative possibilities that accrue to multinationals, however, this can no longer be presupposed. Indeed, Third World development can be retarded more severely than ever before. Moreover, Luxemburg did not see how the colonial imposition of an 'artificial' bourgeoisie or the possibility of an 'alliance' between capitalist and precapitalist class formations could cripple the domestic construction of a capitalist order in an underdeveloped area.

These are all possible criticisms that stem from her approach, but it is interesting that many of the most effective ones at the time came from the social democratic 'left': Otto Bauer, Rudolf Hilferding and, later, Bukharin and Lenin.[14] The thrust of the Austro-Marxist critique was that a marxist analysis did not presume any automatic breakdown, and that it was logically *possible* for capitalism to continue accumulating indefinitely as a 'closed' system. To Lenin's credit, he could maintain his revolutionary perspective without resorting to a breakdown theory. From Luxemburg's standpoint, however, the threat implicit in the Austro-Marxist position was the same as in Bernstein's argument. If capitalism could continue to function indefinitely, the objective underpinning for revolutionary praxis would be undercut. From such a position, she believed that the logical coherence as well as the political necessity of an adamantly anti-imperialist, anti-nationalist, anti-militarist and anti-capitalist perspective would be shattered.

But, there is another reason why Luxemburg did not relinquish her original analysis. Despite the technical problems that many of her critics pointed out, Luxemburg's description of the imperialist process explained what was happening at the time.[15] Whether the *logical necessity* of her essentially uni-causal theory holds in absolute terms or not, it did explicate a real tendency that was in historical operation. Even today, to the extent that imperialism is *a* solution to the capitalist quandary, its practice will necessarily engender militarism and nationalism as Luxemburg claimed.

These were the interconnected tendencies which Luxemburg sought to counteract. Clearly, they formed a spreading cancer which infected both the theory and the practice of the social democratic movement.[16] As one international crisis followed another, as election followed election, as a smouldering nationalism turned into a chauvinist hysteria, the social democratic majority vacillated and compromised itself ever more severely. Such a posture did nothing to halt the tide that would bring on the First World War and the end of an era.

11. War

On 4 August 1914 the Second International turned into 'a stinking corpse'. This was the day on which Rosa Luxemburg's sustained attack on the revisionist drift within social democracy showed itself to have been in vain. It was the day of the SPD's 'great betrayal' of internationalism; the day when it voted for war appropriations to the Kaiser's government.

In making its decision, the party caved in to bourgeois nationalist pressure as well as to the chauvinism that had arisen within its own ranks. Partially from fear of once again being outlaws in a manner reminiscent of the period of the Anti-Socialist laws, partially from sheer opportunism, and partially from a sincere and traditional hatred of Tsarist Russia, the SPD's parliamentary group officially sanctioned the road to slaughter.

In common with other social democratic parties the SPD originally counted upon a quick end to the war. When it dragged on, opposition in the party mounted and, in 1915, 22 SPD Reichstag deputies abstained from voting to extend war credits. Of these 22, 20 left the session. It was this group which formed the nucleus of what would become the Independent Social Democratic Party (USPD). The new party would include people as different as Bernstein, Kautsky, and Zetkin and it is hardly surprising that the USPD was, from the beginning, torn by conflict between those who wanted a radical break from the SPD and those who wished to recreate its old spirit. Indeed, the only real unity within the USPD came from its opposition to the war. A split was inevitable and, in 1916, a minority broke away from the USPD to form the Spartacus League.

Rosa Luxemburg had little direct involvement in these political realignments. She had been thrown into jail shortly after the war began and remained there until its end. But she did experience a tremendous despair at this 'great betrayal' by the

German socialists which she extended to the Second International as a whole. For, to her amazement, the vast majority of her former allies on the left lined up to take sides in the conflict: Jules Guesde, the one time leader of the French socialist left, entered the French War Cabinet; Eduard Vaillant, another major figure on the French left, turned chauvinist; Heinrich Cunow, a theorist and political comrade in the SPD, supported the Germans, and Plekhanov supported the allies. Luxemburg wrote to Camille Huysmans that 'the bankruptcy of the International is as complete as it is terrible.'[1]

While in jail, Luxemburg renewed her assault on the degeneration of international socialism and called for a reckoning with the SPD in a pamphlet, published under the pseudonym 'Junius,' entitled *The Crisis of German Social Democracy*. It became popularly known as the *Junius Pamphlet*, and it created a sensation.

As a polemic, the *Junius Pamphlet* is clearly one of the extraordinary works in the history of socialism and unquestionably Luxemburg's finest stylistic effort. She vents her anger by combining power, drama, lyricism, and reason. Even if only a small taste can be given here, it is still worth savouring:

> The scene has thoroughly changed. The six weeks' march to Paris has become world drama. Mass murder has become a monotonous task, and yet the final solution is not one step nearer. Capitalist rule is caught in its own trap, and cannot ban the spirit that it has invoked . . . The show is over. The curtain has fallen on trains filled with reservists, as they pull out amid the joyous cries of enthusiastic maidens. We no longer see their laughing faces, smiling cheerily from the train windows upon a war-mad population. Quietly they trot through the streets, with their sacks upon their shoulders. And the public, with a fretful face, goes about its daily task. Into the disillusioned atmosphere of pale daylight there rings a different chorus; the hoarse croak of the hawks and hyenas of the battlefield. Ten thousand tents, guaranteed according to specifications, one hundred thousand kilos of bacon, cocoa powder and coffee substitute, and cash on immediate delivery. Shrapnel

drills, ammunition bags, marriage bureaux for war widows, leather belts, war orders – only serious propositions considered. And the cannon fodder that was loaded upon the trains in August and September is now rotting on the battlefields of Belgium and the Vosges, while profits are springing, like weeds, from the fields of the dead.[2]

Luxemburg encapsulates the spirit of the world conflict and powerfully exposes the ideological sophistry that was used to justify the SPD's war policy. On the question of whether the masses would have followed an anti-war policy, she says:

That is a question that no one can answer. But neither is it an important one. Did our parliamentarians demand an absolute assurance of victory from the generals of the Prussian army before voting in favour of war credits? What is true of military armies is equally true of revolutionary armies. They go into the fight, wherever necessity demands it, without previous assurance of success . . . [But, at least] the voice of our party would have acted as a wet blanket on the chauvinistic intoxication of the masses. It would have preserved the intelligent proletariat from delirium, would have made it more difficult for imperialism to poison and to stupefy the minds of the people.[3]

By sticking to its principles, the SPD would have become a rallying point for those opposed to the war. Ideologically and practically, it would have retained its political coherence as well as its traditional commitment to internationalism and peace that had begun symbolically with the courageous opposition of Bebel and Liebknecht to the Franco-Prussian War; thus 'the German proletariat would have remained the lighthouse keeper of socialism and of human emancipation'.[4]

Instead, the SPD proclaimed a policy of 'civil truce' (*Burgfrieden*); the cessation of class struggle for the duration of the war. From Luxemburg's view point, the policy saved no lives and did not 'humanise' the conflict.[5] Rather, it served as an evasion at a time when a real response to the continuation of bourgeois exploitation was needed. For:

What then has changed in this respect when the war broke out? Have private property, capitalist exploitation and class rule ceased to exist? Or have the propertied classes, in a spell of patriotic fervour, declared: in view of the needs of the war we hereby turn the means of production, the earth, the factories and the mills therein, into the possession of the people? Have they relinquished the right to make profits out of these possessions? Have they set aside all political privileges? Will they sacrifice them upon the altar of the fatherland, now that it is in danger?[6]

But the continuation of economic exploitation is not all. In agreeing to the 'civil truce', the SPD condemned itself to accepting virtual martial law: censorship, a ban on the right of assembly and a restriction of public life. It became impossible to awaken the consciousness of the masses and, to this extent, the party abdicated its function.

The question of 'national wars' aside, Luxemburg realised that the question of 'blame' for starting the war was as irrelevant as that of who the 'victor' might be. For Luxemburg, the First World War did not function as a dynamic force to provide the bourgeoisie with the conditions of political 'national' development as wars in the past had done.[7] Thus, questions of 'guilt' or 'victory' would mean little since they could only be decided on the basis of a parasitical, imperialist standpoint in a period when the bourgeoisie had relinquished its progressive role.[8] What becomes necessary then, in the new epoch, is a party which will build 'the readiness of the proletarian masses to act in the fight against imperialism':[9] in short, there is the need to rehabilitate, the old slogan of 'war against war'.[10]

It seems that Rosa Luxemburg thought little of the USPD and was hesitant about the creation of a Spartacus faction. Ultimately, however, she was forced into supporting Spartacus since there was no practical possibility of altering the SPD's course. Besides, the party papers were closed to the left by 1916 while the party aligned itself ever more closely with reactionary militarist groupings which it had originally opposed.

As far as the USPD was concerned, Luxemburg noticed that veterans of the SPD, like Bernstein, Kautsky, Wurm and others, who had led the older party to its degeneration, were members. Furthermore, although ideologically to the left of the SPD, certain members of the USPD were still adamantly opposed to the Russian Revolution despite the fact that the USPD expressed its support for the workers' council movement in Germany.[11]

Of course, Luxemburg's letters from prison do not mention Spartacus because of the censors. Nevertheless, she tried desperately to stay aware of the changing situation. As the war continued, strikes began to take place, led by the Revolutionary Shop Stewards, who were close to the radical elements of the USPD and Spartacus, and carried through by workers in the more radical unions like the metal workers in Berlin. Meanwhile, the SPD was mounting a slanderous and virulent campaign against Spartacus, and especially against its leaders – Rosa Luxemburg and Karl Liebknect – after their release from prison in 1918.

Deprivation and unrest at home, flagging morale at the front, the invasion of Russia, and the threat of defeat in the west – all helped bring the war to a close. In this atmosphere, the bourgeoisie was terrified by the thought of the Russian Revolution spreading to Germany. When the Kaiser abdicated his throne, Philipp Scheidemann – an old revisionist and enemy of Rosa Luxemburg's – proclaimed the Republic that would ultimately be led by Ebert and Noske.[12] This seemingly radical proclamation was, in fact, a counter to Karl Liebknecht's proclamation of a government to be based on the workers' and soldiers' soviets that were being formed both at the front and at home.

Luxemburg supported Liebknecht's proclamation. Emerging emaciated from prison, she immediately began to write articles, make speeches and help publish *Die Rote Fahne* (The Red Flag) while fleeing from one hiding place to another. Yet, she was not uncritical of the revolutionary action of the Berlin proletariat that was inspired by the Spartacists. Not only was she unconvinced of the viability of the Spartacists' revolutionary project, which was completely disorganised and clearly a minority movement among the workers, but she was also doubtful about the possibility of creating a communist party from the Spartacus League.

94

Nevertheless, seeing no alternative, she supported both the formation of the Communist Party of Germany (KPD) in the first days of 1919,[13] and what came to be known as the Spartacus Revolt. Before the Spartacist leadership had even reached a decision on the possibility of revolution, groups of workers invaded the offices of the SPD's newspaper *Vorwärts*. Immediately, Rosa Luxemburg threw her support behind the struggle. Her old belief that one must 'stay in contact with the masses' remained with her, and she paid for it with her life.

In order to stem the revolutionary tide, Ebert and Noske entered into negotiations both with the military and its defeated generals, and with leading industrialists. The result for the 'Weimar' Republic was that the old civil service and judiciary would be retained, private property would not be expropriated and the generals would strive to secure law and order. Thus capitalism survived at the very heart of a new republic headed by socialists; indeed, it was precisely this crucial set of compromises which created the reactionary social infrastructure that would mark the ill-fated 'republic without republicans'.

Once the deal had been made between the old stalwarts of the semi-absolutist state and the SPD, the consequences for the revolutionary left were a foregone conclusion. The Spartacus rebellion was mercilessly crushed. Rosa Luxemburg and Karl Liebknecht were murdered by right-wing soldiers on January 15, 1919 with the tacit consent of Ebert and Noske.

Socialists killed other socialists, and a precedent was set that would haunt the left. Out of the piles of dead revolutionaries, order emerged in the form of the Weimar Republic. In her very last article, Rosa Luxemburg gave her response:

> Order reigns in Berlin! You stupid lackeys! Your 'order' is built on sand. The revolution will raise itself again with clashes, and to your horror it will proclaim with the sound of trumpets: 'I was, I am, I shall be'.[14]

Trumpet calls have been heard in the years that followed, though the completion of the symphony has remained elusive. Nevertheless, in one sense Rosa was right. The order was built on sand and it crumbled in the face of a barbarism the like of which even she could not have foreseen.

12. Rosa Luxemburg and Western Marxism

In the years following her death, both the established social democratic and communist movements have at various times attempted to claim Rosa Luxemburg's legacy only to disclaim it later. This oscillation reflects the impossibility of assimilating her revolutionary thought into either the rigid categories of orthodoxy or the vagaries of reformism. In the truest sense, Luxemburg always stood on the 'left' and it is in this sense that she assumes a preparatory role in the development of an alternative tendency within marxism.

It was Maurice Merleau-Ponty who, in his *Adventures of the Dialectic*, first called this tendency 'western marxism'. Yet, despite the fact that many thinkers of this tendency recognised their indebtedness to her, Luxemburg was given scant attention in this important work. For better or worse, Merleau-Ponty threw together such disparate writers as Trotsky, Lukacs, Korsch and Sartre to define western marxism. Significantly in his *Considerations on Western Marxism*, neither does Perry Anderson concern himself with Luxemburg and he deletes Trotsky from this tendency in the same way that he arbitrarily adds thinkers as varied as Althusser, Colletti, Della Volpe, Lefebvre and the Frankfurt School.

It is, of course, not a question of who should be included and who should be excluded, but of how to assess the tendency. Yet, Anderson's deletion of Trotsky and his refusal to acknowlege the role of Luxemburg or Lenin in the formation of this tendency is indicative. For Anderson wishes to argue that what defines 'western marxism' is its break from the 'classical tradition' as seen in its estrangement from political praxis, its emphasis upon cultural matters, its abstruse use of language, as well as its domination by 'philosophers'.

There is a half-truth to all of this. But, it is always

96

dangerous to take the part for the whole. This is particularly the case once it is recognised that 'western marxism' cannot serve as a rigorous category. In fact, the concept is really only useful in a heuristic sense to define a broad group of leftists who theoretically opposed the dominant perspectives of the two major socialist organisations and who wished to inject new life into a marxism that was becoming ossified into dogma.

Consequently, it is simply missing the point for Anderson to suggest that 'the hidden hallmark of western marxism as a whole is thus that it is a product of defeat'.[1] Of course, it is true that the seminal works of Lukacs and Korsch were published after 1921, that Gramsci wrote his notebooks in prison after the victory of Italian fascism, and that much of the Frankfurt School's work must be seen in terms of the tragedy of Stalinism. But, does this mean that it is necessary to look to the countries of 'actually existing socialism' – with their philosophical sterility and their ideologies of repression – for emancipatory inspiration?

True, the working class has suffered defeats. But, these defeats cannot be ignored by marxist theory. The great works of marxism have never been simply *the product of victory*; rather, they have sought to analyse *the real character of victory*. Thus, marxism, because it is intrinsically tied to a critique of the status quo, cannot make peace with any sort of repression. And, in the period of revolutionary decline, the *original spirit* of western marxism sought to preserve the emancipatory goals inspired by the Russian Revolution. Once these goals were renounced in praxis by both the Soviet Union and the western social democracies, it was inevitable that the western marxists should become estranged from the immediate political praxis. But this does not exhaust the issue. It is in their attempts to break down the barriers of orthodoxy and adapt socialist theory to new conditions and new concerns, that the western marxists have contributed to what Ernst Bloch called 'the underground history of the revolution'.

Only within this context can the similarities between the diverse theorists who comprise this tendency be understood. Thus, in contrast to their more orthodox 'eastern' counterparts,[2] – i.e. Deborin, Bukharin, Preobrazhensky, Zhdanov, Stalin, etc. – the western marxists neither see marxism as an ideology that

97

justifies given forms of repression nor as a 'science' of society. And the reason is not because, as Anderson implies,[3] the western marxists bear a 'hostility' to science but because they believe that marxism neither needs nor retains the truth criteria of the natural sciences.

Instead, like Rosa Luxemburg, the theorists of this tendency interpret marxism as a critical method which is changeable precisely because it must comprehend a changing social reality. As a method, marxism cannot be identified with some positivistic variation of 'reflection theory'.[4] Rather, it seeks to determine the relation between 'moments' of the social 'totality' in terms of a theory of liberation which emphasises the role of class consciousness.

Rosa Luxemburg placed the 'subjective moment' of class consciousness at the very centre of revolutionary action, and it only makes sense that her thought should be situated within this tendency. After all, it was she who most trenchantly showed the insufficiencies within social democratic practice and early Russian communism. Her overriding critique was directed against the bureaucratic tendencies within existing socialist movements, and this kept her from mechanistically identifying the working class with the parties that claimed to represent it.

In her writings, Luxemburg shows a fundamentally critical understanding of the social totality and the role which her party played within it. By the same token, she was heretical in her belief that liberation involved more than freedom from economic want or the seizure of political power by a party. The ability of the mass to participate in the political process, respect for the individual, the development of new forms of social interaction, were always part of her vision.

Though Rosa Luxemburg does not express herself about the philosophical basis for a dialectic of nature, and though, like her contemporaries she often bandies the term 'science' about, the entire thrust of her work and her practical activity indicates that she fundamentally opposed the rigid imposition of external laws upon human activity.[5]

It was always essential to her that the working class understand socio-economic tendencies in terms of the revolutionary goal and, in this respect, Luxemburg would surely have been in agreement with Lukacs' famous statement that class consciousness is the 'ethic' of the proletariat. For Luxemburg, this ethic could only come to fruition through the dialectical interaction of party and mass as a learning process. There would be no absolute primacy for the party in this process, for the goal would involve the development of those self-administrative capabilities of the working class that would make any alienated political forms unnecessary. Thus, Luxemburg structured the discussion of class consciousness in a way that would be developed further by Gramsci, Korsch, and the council communists – many of whom also belong in the tradition of western marxism.

Neither Rosa Luxemburg nor the western marxists started from the assumption that allegiance to marxism meant becoming tied to the statements of a particular text or to specific points of dogma. From their standpoint, marxism could not be conceived as a finished system, but rather as a theory whose purpose lies in developing the working class' understanding of its revolutionary possibilities. In this way, as with Lenin and Trotsky, the role of ideology and class consciousness would ultimately assume a primacy which members of the older social democratic generation did not accord it. As Luxemburg pointedly put the matter, 'in its struggle, the working class has no greater enemy than its own illusions'.[6]

These illusions were precisely what the marxist method was to shatter. In what is probably the crucial text of western marxism, *History and Class Consciousness*, Lukacs would ultimately turn this conception of marxism as a method into the cornerstone of his project. In her analysis of the issue of Polish independence – no less than in *The Accumulation of Capital* – Luxemburg was forced to disagree with specific prescriptions of Marx, Engels and a whole group of socialist intellectual luminaries. Obviously she self-consciously employed the marxist method against Marx himself, thereby placing the method over his own results. In justifying herself, Luxemburg used practically the same words as Lukacs would use later:

Indeed, the essence of 'marxism' lies not in this or that opinion on current questions, but in two basic principles:

99

the dialectical materialist method of historical analysis –
with the theory of class struggle as one of its corollaries –
and Marx's basic analysis of the principles of capitalist
development. The latter theory, which explains the nature
and origin of value, surplus value, money and capital, or
the concentration of capital and capitalist crises, is, strictly
speaking, simply the application – albeit a brilliant one – of
dialectics and historical materialism to the period of
bourgeois economy. Thus, the vital core, the *quintessence*,
of the entire marxist doctrine is the dialectical materialist
method of social enquiry, a method for which no phenomena, or principles, are fixed and unchanging, for which
there is no dogma . . . and for which every historical 'truth'
is subject to a perpetual and remorseless criticism by actual
historical developments.[7]

As a critical method, however, marxism is not simply
confined to criticising 'bourgeois' or 'petty bourgeois' theories.
For, if the existent ideology has its effects on the working
class struggle, and if this ideology is itself shaped by a changing
set of social conditions, then the ideology of marxism itself,
as it is practically and politically employed, must itself be
open to revision in terms of the achievement of its goal. It is in
this sense that Gramsci could speak of marxism as a 'philosophy
of praxis' while Korsch could attempt to strip marxism of its
concerns with metaphysics, highlight its demand for 'dialectical
specificity', and claim that it is necessary to apply the materialist
conception of history to the materialist conception of history
itself.[8]

This is the crux of the matter, and Rosa Luxemburg already
knew it. If marxism is not viewed as a method, it becomes
impossible, from a marxist standpoint, to comprehend and judge
the practice of socialism in terms of the potential emancipation
of the working class. Obviously, such a standpoint retains a
'philosophical' and potentially 'academic' bias which Anderson
and others have criticised. But, the attack on 'intellectualism'
and 'philosophy' *always* leads to authoritarianism as it blunts
criticism and the development of alternatives to the status quo.
For those who rail against 'philosophers' and 'academics,' for

those who decry the break with the 'classical tradition,' it is useful to recall Zinoviev's words – which were directed against 'ultra-leftists' and many who would also be accused of 'Luxemburgism' while standing in the tradition of western marxism – at the Fifth Congress of the Comintern in 1924:

> We will not allow these ultra-leftists to come to the forefront with their revisionism which has already made its appearance internationally. When the Italian comrade Graziadei comes forward with a book in which he re-publishes his old articles that were written while he was still a social democrat and a revisionist, and in which he argues against marxism, we cannot allow such revisionism to go unpunished. When the Hungarian comrade G. Lukacs does the same on a philosophical and sociological plane, we will also not sit by with hands folded . . . [because we will not allow] marxism to be watered down . . . We have a similar tendency in the German Party. Comrade Graziadei is a professor, Korsch is also a professor. (From the Floor: 'Lukacs is a professor as well!') Should another few such professors come forward and promulgate their marxist theories, the situation will become grave indeed. Such theoretical revisionism can neither be condoned nor go unpunished in our Communist International.[9]

It was precisely this attitude which Rosa Luxemburg despised. When she criticised the conservative *Kathedersozialisten* (academic socialists) it was always in political terms. Luxemburg fully recognised the need for theory; she deplored the 'stagnation of marxism' and saw the importance of theoretical innovations in the development of class consciousness.

Because she was so concerned with class consciousness, Luxemburg also understood the need for a continuous criticism of the relation between means and ends as a necessary component of revolutionary activity. Thus, Rosa Luxemburg always put forward the *totality* to be overcome.[10] Whatever the issue which concerned her – whether imperialism, militarism, or nationalism – it would be framed in its relation to the capitalist totality and the growth of a class conscious alternative to it.

Of course, Luxemburg did not fully define this alternative.

101

But, the spirit of her work infuses itself into the development of a method which attempts 'the ruthless criticism of everything existing' (Marx) and which re-asserts the goal of revolutionary democracy. This twin concern has structured the thought of many western marxists as it has been disavowed in practice by the major socialist parties. Precisely to the extent that class consciousness becomes an issue, these early western marxists point to the obstacles that confront the extension of working class control over the whole: i.e. 'reification' 'hegemony', 'subalternity' and so on. In this way, the early western marxists were fostering the demand for a new consciousness – one that would emphasise the active participation of the masses. This project sought to extend the range of social transformation beyond the purely economic and political realms. Hence the development of later western marxists' concerns with cultural and aesthetic questions, the effects of commodity fetishism, the influence of mass culture, and the psychological as well as the philosophical barriers to liberation.

It is true that cultural and epistemological concerns have gained an increased importance in the development of western marxism through the popularity of 'critical theorists' like Adorno, Benjamin and Horkheimer. To deny the importance of their insights would be foolish. If ideology does have an impact on material reality, if consciousness does effect practice, then there will be practical consequencies if bourgeois assumptions are carried over into socialist theory – a point which is crucial to Luxemburg's critique of Bernstein.[11] Furthermore, it is important to understand how capitalism engenders a culture that can blunt the edge of revolutionary consciousness. Finally, with the disaster of Stalinism and Nazism, the threats to individuality cannot be overemphasised.

Of course, it is legitimate to argue that these insights only fit within a new political conception of socialism. But, even in the development of this conception, the Frankfurt School has something to offer. Furthermore, to the same extent that western marxism cannot simply be identified with the Frankfurt School, the Frankfurt School cannot simply be identified with its most popular representatives. Over the years, there have been many who stood in the tradition of western marxism – or who were associated with the Frankfurt Institute of Social Research – who devoted their considerable talents to more directly political concerns which bear a fundamental relevance to any revival of marxist thought. Amongst others: Franz Neumann and Otto Kirchheimer, the great theorists of law and the state; the young Horkheimer, Fromm, and Marcuse who studied the socialising effects of the family; then there are the members of the younger generation like Habermas, Negt and Dutschke who were influenced by older members of the Institute.

There are strong political currents within western marxism – and even within the Frankfurt School circle – which are crucial to the development of a new socialist strategy within and without the major parties. Besides, the argument that alternative tendencies within Marxism have been estranged from praxis is nothing new: Raymond Aron and a host of others have suggested as much, long before Perry Anderson. There are obvious reasons why western marxism has not been accommodated by the major parties, and this has clearly had detrimental effects upon the tendency. Still, the link between theory and practice cannot simply be seen in a mechanistic, immediate, or reductive manner. In the same way that there are anachronistic theories, so are there views which project beyond the status quo and which anticipate emancipatory currents within future movements. Thus, it is not surprising that certain of the most radical elements of the European student revolts of 1968 should have looked to Rosa Luxemburg and the western marxist tradition, or that there is an affinity between her thought and the demands of the Polish workers.

The real issue has nothing to do with a hypostatised notion of praxis. Instead, it revolves around the ability of marxist thought to analyse contemporary tendencies and highlight the emancipatory possibilities within socialism that are ignored in current political practice. The actual danger in contemporary theory lies in the retreat from the project which was formulated by Rosa Luxemburg and many of her theoretical followers.

In this sense, the original western marxists probably stand closer to Luxemburg, Trotsky and even Lenin, than to certain philosophers with whom they have been lumped together. *Certain tendencies* within western marxism have stepped back

103

from Korsch, Lukacs and Gramsci, by substituting a *negative* form of critique for an articulation of the *positive* content of liberation. For example, Adorno's work shows an almost obsessive concern with the abstract freedom of the subject as against the prerequisites for the creation of a society in which the freedom of the individual can be insured and expanded. Again, in many works of Adorno, Horkheimer and Marcuse, a cultural elitism manifests itself which retains anti-democratic overtones and which undermines the construction of real solidarity. Finally, the philosophical pessimism and mysticism that is apparent in much of Benjamin's work as well as certain of Horkheimer's later essays threaten the revolutionary possibilities of speculative social theory. In this sense, a *reversal* within western marxism has occurred which has led to a situation wherein the current possibilities of praxis outstrip the speculative potential within 'critical theory'; as in the case of Poland.

The time has come to *reverse the reversal* – to stop being either 'negative' in Adorno's sense or content with Marcuse's 'great refusal'. There remain pressing issues that demand theoretical confrontation: from the resolution of the organisational contradiction between centralisation and decentralisation to the transformation of a debilitating division of labour, from a new definition of 'efficiency' to the development of new forms of socio-cultural interaction, from the articulation of what constitutes a socialist foreign policy to the development of a viable internationalism that can come to terms with the multi-nationals on the one hand and nationalist provincialism on the other.

There are scores of such issues which demand a non-reformist, unorthodox, solution in terms of the working class and its possibilities for democratic control. The fundamental legacy of Rosa Luxemburg and the most progressive elements within western marxism retains its theoretical power to the extent that the original tendency calls for a reconstitution of these problems in terms of a coherent political project. The rearticulation of this project is the real basis for a renewal of socialist theory that has barely begun.

13. Rosa Luxemburg for the Present

Rosa Luxemburg's thought has not achieved the *stature in praxis* which may be attributed to the theories of Lenin or even Bernstein. In the development of the major socialist movements following her death, the spirit of her thought has lain dormant – though it has, intermittantly, burst forth.

Given the emphasis upon historical 'success' by *both* dogmatic marxists and bourgeois political theorists, Rosa Luxemburg emerges as a courageous, incisive, sincere and idealistic political activist and thinker. As Lenin expressed it in his obituary, she was an 'eagle' who – despite her litany of 'mistakes'[1] – soared above the 'chickens'. That, however, is where it ends – and it is not enough. Indeed, in a sharply critical letter to Konrad Haenisch who had publicly defended her, Rosa Luxemburg warned him 'never to transform political questions into personal, sentimental ones.'[2]

The fact that Rosa Luxemburg was a warm human being of profound sensitivity, a dedicated socialist, and a woman who died a tragic death is not in itself enough to make her relevant to the present. For there have been countless other dedicated socialists, just as warm and just as sensitive, who have died just as tragically. There must be more involved. But, if this dimension is to be uncovered, it is necessary to call into question those assumptions upon which the dominant modes of historical judgments are based.

A fundamental problem occurs when history is viewed purely in terms of the 'successes' it has engendered. Truly, an uncritically examined residue of Hegel's notion that 'the real is rational and the rational is real' comes to be retained in such a view – whether the intellectual debt to Hegel is paid or not. Two questions must then be posed: what about the potential that has not become real? What about the possibilities that have not been actualised?

105

From the traditional perspective these unactualised possibilities and unrealised potentialities for liberation come to be seen as 'irrational'. Consequently, they can be dismissed – but always in the name of the present that has become manifest. In the name of the status quo, the relative validity of unactualised needs and demands that were expressed both in theory and praxis are brushed aside, and termed 'impossible to achieve'.

Of course, since any attempt to achieve these goals is viewed as 'impossible' by definition, a self-fulfilling prophecy results. The ideas and events are then forgotten when history comes to be judged in terms of its practical 'successes' alone. In this way, an ideological benefit for the status quo is assured: the present assumes a purity, a primacy, and a truth which separates it from what lies blood-splattered beneath what Hegel – who at least still retained the tragic sense of historical failure – called 'the slaughterbench of history'. On the other hand, to the extent that those in opposition take on the values of the status quo, they too will rely on the 'tried and tested' rather than exert their imaginations in articulating the new. Co-option is the only logical result precisely because they will judge themselves from the standpoint of 'success', a standpoint that derives only from the vantage point of the present and from the validity that is either consciously or unconsciously given to the status quo. This is why both the west and the east can agree to praise Rosa Luxemburg – and then forget her.

Rosa Luxemburg forces the contemporary left to free its imagination. From her work, it becomes evident that the historical continuum which leads to the present is as little sacrosanct as the present itself. Thus, it becomes necessary to retrieve the elements of a radicalism whose revolutionary content has not been appropriated by the conventional strategies of success and re-establish the real goals of emancipation.

Neutralism and isolationism are not coterminous with internationalism. From Rosa Luxemburg's perspective, socialism and the democratic values of the French Revolution are not limited to one continent, but must be seen in their international possibilities. Of course, the need for tactical compromise will arise. But, these compromises must be understood as such and related to the goal to be achieved. In this sense, Rosa Luxemburg's emphasis upon making the conceptual connection between immediate needs and ultimate goals is the cornerstone of any reconstruction of socialist theory and praxis.

Throughout her work there is the reminder that imperialism cannot be overcome without a simultaneous attack upon its progenitor: capitalism. Following Marx, Luxemburg always understood that to be radical is 'to go to the root', that is to say, to the *actual structural conditions* of capitalism that make imperialism possible and necessary. Beyond the liberal guilt, the naive beliefs in 'cultural identity,' or the ill-conceived ideas of 'cultural relativism,' which so often cloud the political judgments of the left, an implicit lesson emerges from Rosa Luxemburg's work: the *fundamental* emphasis upon imperialism and anti-colonialism can obscure class divisions within the colonised themselves. It is no wonder then that, where nationalism becomes the sole imperialist battle cry, capitalism should surface once again and that wars among the oppressed nations should become a commonplace.

Rosa Luxemburg makes the left cognizant of the fact that there can be no theoretical compromise regarding what it opposes and what it supports, whether a movement chooses to call its ideology 'socialist' or not, 'liberating' or not. She recognised that the basic ideological emphasis upon nationalism, dead traditions, religion, sex, or race, would only lead to a lack of clarity about the basis upon which contemporary oppression is grounded. As she writes again and again, only when national goals – or any particularist goals – become concommitant 'with the solidarity of the proletariat' does the actual potential for liberation from the structural conditions of capitalism arise.

Reflecting upon these structural conditions and judging what will strengthen the 'solidarity of the proletariat', without compromising its class consciousness, is what demands the exercise of the critical faculty – and the critical faculty does not mature through the repetition of dogma. From her youth, Luxemburg understood that it was Marx's method, not any one of his particular judgments, that provided the key to emancipation. Whilst she would never neglect the emancipatory goals of marxism, Luxemburg also realised that the present cannot be judged in terms of some abstract ideal. It was this which served as the basis for her profound distrust of sectarianism and, simultaneously, for her belief in the need for theory to clarify that ideal within the practical possibilities of the existing situation.

In the manifestation of the goal within everyday politics, critical theory necessarily becomes part of political activity. Thus, Luxemburg's central concern is that the critical faculty be fostered in those masses who are the prime victims and targets of their oppressors' ideology. From Luxemburg's life work, it becomes clear that there is no substitute for such activity which necessitates staying 'in contact with the masses' through helping to develop a political organisation. But such an organisation is not an end unto itself. The real end is nothing other than the self-administration of the masses.

In Luxemburg's view, everything that stands in the way of the masses' attempts to control their own destiny needs to be specified and overcome. But she also realised that insofar as the mass must exercise power, it must simultaneously *learn* to exercise it. Clearly this must be done through politics, through participating in the development of an organisation that is dedicated to building the masses' recognition of their own creative powers and their own potential for control. Such is the dialectic that informs the relation between organisation and mass in her vision. Only as the revolutionary consciousness of the masses grows and then culminates in action does the differentiation between the two dissolve into new forms of social interaction.

Luxemburg therefore becomes the virtual progenitor of a tendency within marxism that seeks to oppose all types of bureaucratic formalism. For her, the essential element in a working class party was the radicalisation of consciousness and socialisation of knowledge that would, *as part of the process*, undermine the need for hierarchical leadership to infuse class solidarity. This can never be done through distortions, lies, claims for a supposed proletarian infallibility, conspiracy theories, babytalk, or bellicosity – all of which are practised either by established communist regimes or the various sects in America and elsewhere. For Rosa, the working class always has to know the truth and learn from its mistakes. Only in this way can the *process* develop by which the working class will enter 'the school of public life' and create a viable socialist culture.

108

From this standpoint, the purpose of the party lies in creating the conditions for its own disappearance through deepening the radical tradition of theory and practice, even in periods of revolutionary decline. In this way, the long term project unfolds: the transformation of politics itself from a set of activities which is external to the individual to a practice that is essential to his or her own development as a member of a socialist community.

Such a development demands a new discussion of the concepts of freedom and responsibility. Freedom cannot simply remain internal or negative. Rather, it must become positive – in the sense of Hegel and Marx – to the extent that reciprocal obligations come to be delineated in social and political terms. This type of positive freedom will ultimately bring democracy to the foreground of socialism to the same degree that it will attack bureaucratic formalism.

Let there be no mistake: the merger of socialism and democracy does not sanction the right to appropriate the profits produced by the labour of others. Such a right would necessarily leave freedom in the abstract for the majority of the people. For Rosa Luxemburg, the point is precisely to create the conditions in which democracy can be extended from the formal freedoms of bourgeois representative government into the actual relations of everyday life in civil society.

Rosa Luxemburg re-affirms the goal of socialism which has been lost sight of all too often. It is the goal of a freedom that remains to be attained, a practical freedom which ultimately calls for the democratic control of the process of production as well as the distribution of wealth. For Luxemburg, the freedoms that have been won cannot simply be discarded or abolished; they must be deepened. This is why, in opposition to the Bolsheviks, she wrote the famous lines:

> Freedom only for the supporters of the government, only for the members of one party – however numerous they may be – is no freedom at all. Freedom is always and exclusively freedom for the one who thinks differently. Not because of any fanatical concept of 'justice', but because all that is instructive, wholesome, and purifying in political

freedom depends on this essential characteristic, and its effectiveness vanishes when 'freedom' becomes a special privilege.[3]

In this respect, Rosa Luxemburg implicitly calls for a *socialist tolerance* that has been absent all too long. This is only possible in the practice of democracy and, indeed, it is only through this practice that the goal of freedom becomes manifest. This is an insight that was lost amidst the carnage of Stalinism. From her work, it becomes evident that freedom cannot exist in the abstract, but must always mean a freedom to expand the horizon of possibilities within a non-exploitive society.

Only once the concepts of freedom and democracy are viewed as unfinished, as a process, does the revolutionary goal emerge. For Rosa Luxemburg, freedom is not a fixed condition and democracy is not confined to one government, state, or economic system. Indeed, Luxemburg dispelled the illusion that there is an intrinsic relation between capitalism and democracy, which only makes the preservation and extension of democratic liberties that much more essential against threats from the right or groups that foster slogans without content and ideologies without vision. For a socialist movement, democracy is the internal means and the external end; where true socialism is impossible without democracy, true democracy is impossible without socialism. Though there may be practical exigencies that cannot be ignored, Luxemburg continually warned against allowing any temporary measures to be turned into high points of dogma. In this respect, her criticism of the SPD's 'parliamentary cretinism' was not very different from her critique of Bolshevism. She always saw moments of expediency and compromise in terms of their potential effects on the conquest of political power by, and the ultimate goals of, the working class.

Indeed, the most daring element of Luxemburg's legacy involves the continual reminder that a new society must be placed on the socialist agenda. Yet, the new remains indeterminate, open and structured only by the accumulation of contradictions in the present as well as by what can be learned from the past. There can be no simple dichotomy between the tasks of the present and the reconciliation of these contradictions in terms of the final goal. Stalinism has shown all too well how the socialist goal can be continually pushed into an ever-receding future in the name of the immediate tasks of the present, once this rigid split is made. But such a dichotomy between present and future is not only attributable to Stalinism, it is part of reformist social democratic tactics as well. The liquidation of socialism as an *alternative* to capitalism through the emphasis upon particular reforms *per se* has resulted in an identity crisis for social democracy that can only be theoretically mitigated through a re-evaluation of the left's most revolutionary proponents in terms of contemporary needs. For overcoming this crisis will require raising currently untouchable questions ranging from the transformation of the hierarchical division of labour to the development of a new socialist culture.

Naturally, there is not just one set of demands to guide the working class in all situations and at all times. But, at least, the outlines of the socialist project must be made clear in its universal implications: the creation of democratic forms to allow the working class to determine its needs and goals. Democracy becomes its own end where the masses themselves take this responsibility – initially with regard to what is produced and how it is to be distributed. But that is only the beginning. As democracy becomes the object of study in the 'school of public life', perhaps a renaissance, a many-sidedness, will develop in people's lives – a many-sidedness and broadness of interest that is itself prefigured in the life of this extraordinary woman, Rosa Luxemburg.

In her politics and her life, the other tradition, the forgotten tradition, of marxism begins. As the left starts to make use of that tradition in informing its theory and practice, perhaps we will begin to see the meaning of what Marx meant when he enigmatically wrote:

> the world has long had a dream of something which it only has to conceptualise consciously to possess in actuality. Then it will become evident that there is not simply an empty space between past and future, but rather that it is a matter of *realising* the thoughts of the past.

References

1. Childhood and Youth pp. 13–16

1 At the end of her life, Luxemburg expressed herself to Mathilde Wurm in one of her most beautiful letters:

> What do you want with this particular suffering of the Jews? The poor victims on the rubber plantations in Putamayo, the Negroes in Africa with whose bodies the Europeans play a game of catch, are just as near to me. Do you remember the words written on the work of the Great General Staff about Trotha's campaign in the Kalahari desert? 'and the death-rattles, the mad cries of those dying of thirst, faded away into the sublime silence of eternity'.
>
> Oh, this 'sublime silence of eternity' in which so many screams have faded away unheard. It rings within me so strongly that I have no special corner of my heart reserved for the ghetto: I am at home wherever in the world there are clouds, birds and human tears.

S. E. Bronner (ed.), *The Letters of Rosa Luxemburg*, Boulder, Colorado, 1979, pp. 179–180.

2 *ibid.* p. 227.

3 J. P. Nettl, *Rosa Luxemburg*, 2 vols, London, 1966, p. 45.

4 *ibid.* p. 63ff.

5 See Elzbieta Ettinger (ed.), *Comrade and Lover: Rosa Luxemburg's Letters to Leo Jogiches*, London, Pluto 1981.

6 R. Luxemburg, 'Der Sozialpatriotismus in Polen' (Social patriotism in Poland) in *Gesammelte Werke* 1/1, p. 50.

7 R. Luxemburg, 'Strömungen in der polnischen sozialistischen Bewegung' (Tendencies in the Polish socialist movement) in *Gesammelte Werke* 1/1, p. 18.

8 J. Braunthal, *History of the International*, 2 vols, trans. by H. Collins and K. Mitchell, New York, 1967, vol. 1, p. 231.

2. Nationalism and Internationalism pp. 17–23

1 Compare with: 'The Communist Manifesto' in K. Marx and F. Engels, *Selected Works*, 3 vols, Moscow, 1969, vol. 1, pp. 116–18.

2 R. Luxemburg, 'The national question and autonomy' in H. B. Davis (ed.), *The National Question: Selected Writings by Rosa Luxemburg*, New York, 1976, p. 101.

3 R. Luxemburg, 'Foreword to the anthology *The Polish Question and the Socialist Movement*' in *The National Question*, p. 63.

4 *ibid.* p. 85.

5 R. Luxemburg, 'The Junius pamphlet: the crisis in German social democracy' in M. A. Waters (ed.), *Rosa Luxemburg Speaks*, New York, 1970, pp. 307ff.

6 Lenin's basic writings on the national question are handily collected in V. I. Lenin, *National Liberation, Socialism and Imperialism: Selected Writings*, New York, 1968.

7 In his essay, 'The discussion on self-determination summed up', Lenin takes great pains to distinguish his position from that of the old economistic marxists by arguing that the socialist organisation of production will give 'full play' to the 'sympathies' of national populations and thereby draw them into a larger organisation. *ibid.* p. 129. Lenin also notes how it is actually the internationalisation of capital which will make this possible and desirable. Thus, in his 'Critical remarks on the national question', he writes:

> Marxism cannot be reconciled with nationalism, be it even of the 'most just', 'purest' most refined and civilised brand. In place of all forms of nationalism, marxism advances internationally the amalgamation of all nations in the higher unity, a unity that is growing before our eyes with every mile of railway line that is built, with every international trust and every workers' association that is formed (an association that is international in its economic activities as well as in its ideas and aims).

ibid. p. 27.

8 *ibid.* pp. 27–8.

9 *ibid.* p. 27.

10 See: O. Bauer, *Die Nationalitätenfrage und die Sozialdemo-*

kratie. (The Question of the Nationalities and Social Democracy), Vienna, 1907.

11 J. V. Stalin, 'Marxism and the national question' in *Works*, vol. 2 (1907–13) Moscow, 1953.

12 After the failure of the European revolts of 1918–21, Lenin and the majority of the Bolsheviks faced the fact that, temporarily at least, they would have to survive in one country. Though Lenin continued to oppose 'Great Russian chauvinism', and stressed the international aspect, there is a link between his views and Stalin's later theory of nationalism, despite the difference of contexts.

13 See F. Claudin, *The Communist Movement: From Comintern to Cominform*, 2 vols, New York, 1975.

14 R. Luxemburg, 'The national question and autonomy' in *The National Question*, pp. 135–36.

15 *ibid.* p. 102.

16 *ibid.* p. 135.

17 The duty of the class party of the proletariat to protest and resist national oppression arises not from any special 'right of nations', just as, for example, its striving for the social and political equality of sexes does not at all result from any special 'rights of women' which the movement of bourgeois emancipation refers to. This duty arises solely from the general opposition to every form of social inequality and social domination, in a word, from the basic position of socialism. *ibid.*

18 Ultimately, even here, Lenin and Luxemburg would disagree on the type of International involved. Thus, following the collapse of the Second International in the face of the first world war, Luxemburg believed that the organisation should be revamped rather than supplanted by a Third International which, she prophesied, would be dominated by the Soviet Union.

3. A Revolutionary in the West: The Party in Context pp. 24–30

1 Arthur Rosenberg shows beautifully how Marx and Engels never completely understood the real character of the new

European labour parties that developed after 1863. Indeed, Rosenberg suggests that on every specific issue of consequence – ranging from internationalism to war, from the industrial proletariat to the Russian and economic questions such as free trade vs. protectionism – the disciples were at odds with the prophets. A. Rosenberg, *Democracy and Socialism: A Contribution to the Political History of the Past 150 Years*, trans. G. Rosen, London, 1939, pp. 295–96ff.

2 From 1881, when it polled 311,961 votes, the SPD grew to amass 1,427,298 votes in 1890. In 1887 it received 10.1 per cent of the Reichstag election vote, and by 1903 the party had attracted over three million voters and 31.7 percent of the vote. C. E. Schorske, *German Social Democracy 1905–1917: The Development of the Great Schism*, New York, 1972 edn, pp. 387.

3 In this regard, see: H. U. Wehler, *Das deutsche Kaiserreich 1871–1918*, Göttingen, 1973, pp. 41–60; and M. Kitchen, *The Political Economy of Germany 1815–1914*, Montreal, 1978.

4 See: M. Salvadori, *Karl Kautsky and the Socialist Revolution 1880–1938* trans. by Jon Rothschild, London, 1979.

5 For the philosophical criticisms of the Kautskyian brand of mechanistic marxism, see K. Korsch, *Marxism and Philosophy*, trans. F. A. Halliday, London, 1970 and G. Lukacs, *History and Class Consciousness: Studies in Marxist Dialectics*, trans. R. Livingstone, Cambridge, 1971. Also, see Lenin's *The Proletarian Revolution and the Renegade Kautsky* and Korsch's *Die materialistische Geschichtsauffassung: Eine Auseinandersetzung mit Karl Kautsky*. (The Materialist Conception of History: A Controversy with Karl Kautsky), Leipzig, 1929.

6 Though Rosa Luxemburg disliked the work, August Bebel's autobiography provides a clear picture of social democratic life and a wealth of information. A. Bebel, *Aus meinem Leben* (From My Life), 3 vols, Stuttgart, 1910–1914. See also H. Hirsch, *August Bebel*, Koln, 1968.

7 J. Braunthal, *History of the International*, 2 vols, trans by H. Collins and K. Mitchell, New York, 1967, vol. 1, p. 200.

8 *ibid.* p. 270.

9 *ibid.* p. 267.

10 G. Lichtheim, *Marxism: An Historical and Critical Study*, New York, 1961, p. 263.

11 The foolishness of this idea regarding the 'passivity' of the masses which was supposedly induced by viewing marxism as a 'science' that would guarantee the triumph of socialism cannot be overemphasised. It was Lassalle who spoke of 'science behind the masses'; the socialist organisations did not grow through inactivity, but through building up the class consciousness of the masses by hard work. This consciousness was *always* a crucial factor, and it was expressed in the cultural world which social democracy created for its members – what the Austrians would call an *Arbeiterwelt*. Journals, satirical weeklies, comic books, party schools, choir groups, conferences, discussion sections, sports events and other activities were all supported by socialist parties throughout Europe in order to build up the socialist consciousness of the masses; See: J. Joll, *The Second International, 1889–1914*, New York, 1966, p. 65. It is mistaken to view the failure of the Second International simply in terms of its ideology of objectivism. The far more important issue involved the emphasis upon reformism by the trade unions and a Reichstag delegation that became increasingly insulated from the masses as the party grew. Thus, reformism came to be buttressed by an organisational petrification which narrowed politics to the matter of immediate reforms and which truncated the 'socialist public sphere' by separating politics from the cultural education process of the workers themselves. This development has been discerned as happening long before 1914 in Robert Michels' classic study, *Political Parties*, trans. E. & C. Paul, New York, 1962.

13 Bronner, *The Letters of Rosa Luxemburg*, Boulder, Colorado, 1979, p. 84.

4. Revisionism and Orthodoxy pp. 31–40

1 In this regard, the English title *Evolutionary Socialism* trans. E. C. Harvey, New York, 1961, is misleading. The German title translates as: The Presuppositions of Socialism and the Tasks of Social Democracy (*Die Voraussetzungen des Sozialismus und die Aufgaben der Sozialdemokratie*) and gives a far better sense of Bernstein's undertaking.

2 The dismay over Bernstein's 'defection' in leading party circles cannot be overemphasised. The respect that Bernstein had earned gave rise to numerous pleas that he abandon his position and return to the fold; the most famous of which was probably that of Ignaz Auer which contained the lines: 'my dear Ede, the things of which you speak are not things which are talked about, they are things which are done'. Indeed, it was probably in part the extraordinary respect which was accorded him that kept Bernstein from being expelled; as Victor Adler put it 'social democracy must always have a place for a man like Ede'. See: F. Adler (hrs.), *Victor Adler's Briefwechsel mit August Bebel und Karl Kautsky*, (Victor Adler's Correspondence with August Bebel and Karl Kautsky), Vienna, 1954, pp. 257ff.

3 K. Korsch, 'The passing of marxian orthodoxy: Bernstein – Kautsky – Luxemburg – Lenin' in D. Kellner (ed.), *Karl Korsch: Revolutionary Theory*, Austin, Texas, 1977, p. 177.

4 E. Bernstein 'Wie ist wissenschaftlicher sozialismus möglich' (How is scientific socialism possible?) in H. Hirsch (ed.), *Ein Revisionistisches Sozialismusbild: Drei Vorträge* (A Revisionist View of Socialism: Three Essays), Hannover, 1966.

5 R. Luxemburg, 'Social reform or revolution', in D. Howard (ed.), *Selected Political Writings of Rosa Luxemburg*, New York, 1971, p. 89.

6 In this regard, see Luxemburg's critique of Max Schippel and the debate about militarism which appeared as an appendix to the second edition of 'Social reform or revolution' in Howard's anthology.

7 See: N. Geras, *The Legacy of Rosa Luxemburg*, London, 1976, p. 116. Geras oversimplifies the matter when he claims that Luxemburg could offer no alternative policy.

8 Luxemburg, 'Social reform or revolution', pp. 60–61.

9 *ibid.* p. 67.

10 *ibid.* p. 70.

11 For [Rosa Luxemburg] history is not linear but proceeds by dialectical contradictions via the class struggle. As we have seen, historical necessity does exist in the sense that history cannot be made arbitrarily, it is not a business where you can buy what you want but where the present always conditions the future. Nevertheless, since this present is always contradictory the present society is torn by class conflict, it contains contradictory trends; imperialism and socialism are both objective tendencies of the development of society. For that reason, if you want the socialist trend of historical development to prevail over the other, you must fight hard at every stage, but you must do it in a rigorously scientific way, that is to say you must first analyse the objective trends of the development of society, isolate their revolutionary elements, and press forward strongly in that direction in such a way as to increase both the conflict with the ruling class (which is of necessity pulling the development of society in the opposite direction) as well as the revolutionary consciousness of the masses.

L. Basso, *Rosa Luxemburg: A Reappraisal*, trans. D. Parmee, New York, 1975, p. 58–9.
12 Luxemburg, 'Social reform or revolution', p. 109.
13 *ibid.* p. 83.
14 *ibid.* pp. 85, 87.
15 *ibid.* p. 115.
16 *ibid.*
17 *ibid.* p. 116.
18 See: A. Przeworski, 'Social democracy as a historical phenomenon' in *New Left Review*, 122, July 1980.
19 Luxemburg, 'Social reform or revolution,' p. 121.
20 R. Luxemburg, 'Erorterungen uber die taktik' in *Gesammelte Werke* 1/1, pp. 257–8.
21 Luxemburg, 'Social reform or revolution,' pp. 105–6.
22 *ibid.* pp. 72–73.
23 *ibid.* p. 105.
24 R. Luxemburg, 'Kautsky's Buch Wider Bernstein' in *Gesammelte Werke* 1/1, p. 546.
25 J. Braunthal, *History of the International*, 2 vols, trans. H. Collins and K. Mitchell, New York, 1967, vol. 1, pp. 270–71.

5. Intermezzo: Rosa Luxemburg and the Cultural Milieu of Social Democracy pp. 41–48

1 This was particularly evident in what amounted to a Schiller cult within the SPD. Although Engels himself was President of the *Schiller Verein* in Manchester, many – including Luxemburg and Franz Mehring – felt that the attempt to adopt Schiller would dilute the project of social transformation by the injection of sentimentalism. In this regard, the manner in which Herbert Marcuse refers to the Schiller of *The Letters on the Aesthetic Education of Man* in his most utopian work: *Eros and Civilization*, (Boston, 1969) is interesting.

2 Aside from Mehring's *The Lessing Legend*, an indicative work is Plekhanov's *Art and Social Life*.

3 The various attempts to evaluate the avant-garde from the standpoint of the left would culminate in the famous 'expressionist debates' whose principle participants were Lukacs, Bloch and Brecht. In this regard, see my forthcoming essay 'Expressionism and Marxism: towards an aesthetic of emancipation' in S. E. Bronner and D. Kellner (eds.), *Passion and Rebellion: The Expressionist Heritage*.

4 S. E. Bronner, *The Letters of Rosa Luxemburg*, Boulder, Colorado, 1979, p. 228.

5 R. Luxemburg, 'Tolstoi als sozialer Denker' in *Gesammelte Werke* 2, pp. 246–54.

6 See: A. Tertz's essay in *The Trial Begins*, and *On Socialist Realism* trans. M. Hayward, New York, 1960, where art is seen as subordinate to the specific needs of political policy. It is in this that Tertz sees the kernel of the Soviet attempt to turn art into propaganda.

7 R. Luxemburg, 'The spirit of Russian literature: life of Korolenko' in M. Waters (ed.), *Rosa Luxemburg Speaks*, New York, 1970, p. 342.

8 *ibid.* p. 346.

9 Bronner, *The Letters of Rosa Luxemburg*, p. 253.

10 *ibid.* p. 180.

11 Luxemburg, 'The spirit of Russian literature', p. 348.

12 Bronner, *The Letters of Rosa Luxemburg*, pp. 237–8.

6. The East European Dimension pp. 49–57

1 S. E. Bronner, *The Letters of Rosa Luxemburg*, Boulder, Colorado, 1979, p. 79.

2 A. Rosenberg, *Democracy and Socialism: A Contribution to the Political History of the Past 150 years*, trans. G. Rosen, London, 1939, pp. 330–33.

3 For some fine insights, see the chapter entitled 'Before and after the 1905 revolution' in the forthcoming book by Raya Dunayevskaya, *Rosa Luxemburg, Women's Liberation and Marx's Philosophy of Revolution*.

4 R. Luxemburg, 'The organizational question of social democracy', in D. Howard (ed.) *Selected Political Writings of Rosa Luxemburg*, New York, 1971, p. 387.

5 *ibid*. p. 289.

6 *ibid*.

7 R. Luxemburg, 'Mass strike, party, and trade unions' in *ibid*. p. 264.

8 In this regard, see the superficial and dogmatic Leninist argument forwarded by J. Molyneux, *Marxism and the Party*, London, 1978, p. 116.

9 Luxemburg, 'The organizational question of social democracy', p. 304.

10 For an overview of the various positions on the mass strike debate, see Karl Kautsky, *Der Politische Massenstreik* (The Political Mass Strike), Berlin, 1914.

11 J. P. Nettl, *Rosa Luxemburg*, 2 vols, London, 1966, vol. 1, p. 301.

12 Bronner, *The Letters of Rosa Luxemburg*, p. 114.

7. The Revolutions in Russia: Democracy and Mass Strike pp. 58–67

1 S. E. Bronner (ed.), *The Letters of Rosa Luxemburg*, Boulder, Colorado, 1979, p. 95.

2 C. E. Schorske, *German Social Democracy 1905–1917: The Development of the Great Schism*, New York, 1972 edn, pp. 89ff.

3 R. Luxemburg, 'Mass strike, party and trade unions', in D.

Howard (ed.) *Selected Political Writings of Rosa Luxemburg*, New York, 1971, p. 240.

4 *ibid.* p. 252.

5 *ibid.* p. 249.

6 *ibid.* p. 247.

7 *ibid.* p. 237.

8 *ibid.*

9 Thus, during the war, Luxemburg noted ruefully: 'How we fancied ourselves strong, how we boasted of our four million supporters before the war, and yet how our strength folded at the first test, like a house of cards.' R. Luxemburg, 'Either/or' in *ibid.* p. 345.

10 Bronner (ed.), *The Letters of Rosa Luxemburg*, p. 123.

11 *ibid.*

12 Her response to Kautsky on this matter led to their ultimate break. The essential part of her response may be found in R. Luxemburg, *Theory and Practice*, trans. D. Wolff, Detroit, 1980.

13 The most cogent rejoinder to Luxemburg is the essay by G. Lukacs, 'Critical observations on Rosa Luxemburg's "Critique of the Russian revolution"' in *History and Class Consciousness: Studies in Marxist Dialectics*, trans. R. Livingstone, London, 1971.

14 R. Luxemburg, 'The Russian Revolution', in M. Waters (ed.), *Rosa Luxemburg Speaks*, New York, 1970, p. 378.

15 *ibid.* p. 377.

16 *ibid.* p. 381.

17 *ibid.* p. 382.

18 *ibid.* p. 380.

19 *ibid.* p. 385.

20 *ibid.* pp. 390–91.

21 Thus, in Russia, the point could be argued in terms of the possibility for democracy as such; the immediate choice did not have to be made between bourgeois democracy and the soviets. On the other hand, the events of 1919 in Germany were fundamentally determined by choosing between *either* soviets or a parliament in the most immediate way. Luxemburg's allegiance to the Spartacus group at that time obviously led her to opt for the soviets since it was readily apparent that the new parliament, which would enshrine the Weimar Republic, would be socioeconomically based upon a perilous compromise between the social democrats and the most reactionary forces in Germany.

22 J. P. Nettl, *Rosa Luxemburg*, 2 vols, London 1966, vol 2, p. 718.
23 Luxemburg, 'The Russian Revolution', p. 391.
24 *ibid.* p. 393.
25 *ibid.* p. 394.
26 Bronner (ed.), *The Letters of Rosa Luxemburg*, p. 258.
27 Luxemburg, 'The Russian Revolution' p. 395.

8. Correspondence: Friends and Lovers pp. 68–76

1 These letters to Mathilde Jacob, along with some interesting reflections by her, are collected in Charlotte Beradt (ed.), *Rosa Luxemburg im Gefängnis*, Frankfurt, 1973.
2 The two editions of letters which came out shortly after her death, as well as Roland-Holst's biography which appeared in the midst of Stalinism, served to emphasise the humanism of the great revolutionary. See: *Briefe aus dem Gefängnis*, Berlin, 1920; *Briefe an Karl und Luise Kautsky* (1896–1918), Berlin, 1923; and *Letters to Karl and Luise Kautsky* (trans. L. P. Lockner) New York, 1923; also, Roland-Holst's *Rosa Luxemburg. Haar leven en werken*, Rotterdam, 1935.
3 J. P. Nettl, *Rosa Luxemburg*, 2 vols, London, 1966, vol. 1, p. 14.
4 Luxemburg 'The organizational question of social democracy' in D. Howard (ed.), *Selected Political Writings of Rosa Luxemburg*, New York, 1971, pp. 303–4.
5 S. E. Bronner, *The Letters of Rosa Luxemburg*, Boulder, Colorado, 1979, p. 178.
6 *ibid.* pp. 241–2.

9. The Socialist Left – On the Defensive pp. 77–82

1 J. Braunthal, *History of the International*, 2 vols, trans. H. Collins and K. Mitchell, New York, 1967, vol. 1, p. 301.
2 L. Basso, *Rosa Luxemburg: A Reappraisal*, trans. D. Parmee, New York, 1975, p. 79.

3 See: 'Social democracy and parliamentarism' in R. Looker, (ed.), *Rosa Luxemburg: Selected Political Writings*, New York, 1974.

4 See O. Negt's brilliant essay, 'Rosa Luxemburg, zur materialistischen dialektik von spontaneität und organisation' in C. Pozzoli (ed.), *Rosa Luxemburg oder Die Bestimmung des Sozialismus*, Frankfurt, 1974.

5 For a fine overview of the development of bureaucratic tendencies in the SPD see: C. E. Schorske, *German Social Democracy 1905-1917: The Development of the Great Schism*, New York, 1972 edn, pp. 118-46.

6 *ibid.* pp. 23, 7.

7 Neither the right nor the left actually understood the implications and contradictions of a concept such as world war. It was a lack of imagination for which the International would later pay a heavy price. Indeed, Rosenberg makes the fascinating point that the famous peace resolution actually hindered the policy formation of the SPD since it condemned the Party to a pacifist position which would prove politically ineffective. A. Rosenberg, *Democracy and Socialism: A Contribution to the Political History of the Past 150 years*, trans G. Rosen, London, 1939, pp. 309ff.

8 See Luxemburg's controversial 'Concerning Morocco' in D. Howard (ed.), *Selected Political Writings of Rosa Luxemburg*, New York, 1971.

9 Schorske, *German Social Democracy 1905-1917* pp. 177-81.

10 R. Luxemburg, 'Was weiter?' in *Gesammelte Werke* Bd. 2. pp. 288-99. The essay is translated in Looker's anthology *Selected Political Writings* as 'The next step'.

11 See the fine discussion in the chapter entitled 'The break with Kautsky, 1910-1911' in R. Dunayevskaya's forthcoming book, *Rosa Luxemburg, Women's Liberation and Marx's Philosophy of Revolution*.

12 Because the demand for a republic was associated with the SPD, though never officially part of the program, it could be brought to the forefront or neglected by various factions at various times as the circumstances dictated.

13 R. Luxemburg, *Theory and Practise*, trans. D. Wolff, *News and Letters*, 1980, p. 8 and *passim*.

10. Imperialism pp. 83–89

1   The bourgeoisie, by the rapid improvement of all instruments of production, by the immensely facilitated means of communication, draws all, even the most barbarian, nations into civilisation. The cheap prices of its commodities are the heavy artillery with which it batters down all Chinese walls, with which it forces the barbarians' intensely obstinate hatred of foreigners to capitulate. It compels all nations, on pain of extinction, to adopt the bourgeois mode of production: it compels them to introduce what it calls civilisation into their midst, i.e. to become bourgeois themselves. In one word, it creates a world after its own image.

'The Communist Manifesto', in K. Marx and F. Engels, *Selected Works*, 3 vols, Moscow, 1969, vol. 1, p. 112.

2   Thus the immediate and vital condition for capital and its accumulation is the existence of non-capitalist buyers of the surplus value, which is decisive to this extent for the problem of capitalist accumulation. Whatever the theoretical aspects, the accumulation of capital, as an historical process, depends in every respect upon non-capitalist social strata and forms of social organisation.

R. Luxemburg, *The Accumulation of Capital*, trans. A. Schwarzschild, New York, 1968, p. 366.

3   Hence the contradictory phenomena that the old capitalist countries provide ever larger markets for, and become increasingly dependent upon, one another, yet on the other hand compete ever more ruthlessly for trade relations with non-capitalist countries. Imperialism itself can then be defined in terms of the economic struggle of these interdependent capitalist countries against one another for precapitalist territories.

ibid, pp. 367, 446.

4 *ibid*. pp. 416 ff.

5 N. Geras, *The Legacy of Rosa Luxemburg*, London, 1976, p. 16; his discussion of this theme is excellent.

6 This, of course, is the Stalinist version of 'Luxemburgism'. For

more on 'Luxemburgism' see: J. P. Nettl, *Rosa Luxemburg*, 2 vols, London, 1966, vol. 2, pp. 787ff.

7 S. E. Bronner (ed.), *The Letters of Rosa Luxemburg*, Boulder, Colorado, 1979, p. 104.

8 The vacillation within the Second International really began with the publication of Shaw's *Fabianism and the Empire* which justified the British annexation of the Boer Republic in 1900. By 1904, at the Amsterdam Congress, van Kol's resolution condemned imperialism even though 'we do not consider that it is necessarily bad for a country to be colonised in any circumstances'. The resolution was passed with the support of Bernstein, who had already given a certain support to imperialism in *Evolutionary Socialism*. By 1907, the issue of imperialism was already polarising the International and, by 1910, the collapse of the left on the issue was already foreseeable. J. Braunthal, *History of the International*, 2 vols, trans. H. Collins and K. Mitchell, New York, 1967, vol. 1, pp. 306–19.

9 See: *Theory and Practice*, trans. D. Wolff, Detroit, 1980, where Luxemburg condemns the butchery of von Trotha's troops and praises the anti-colonial native rebels. This is only one example among many.

10 Nettl, p. 837.

11 See: Luxemburg, 'Militia and militarism', in D. Howard (ed.), *Selected Political Writings of Rosa Luxemburg*, New York, 1971.

12 L. Basso, *Rosa Luxemburg: A Reappraisal*, trans. D. Parmee, New York, 1975, pp. 44ff.

13 See: 'Peace utopias' in M. Waters (ed.), *Rosa Luxemburg Speaks*, New York, 1970.

14 Luxemburg responded to these early critics in her *The Accumulation of Capital – An Anti-Critique*, New York, 1972.

15 G. Lichtheim, *Marxism: An Historical and Critical Study*, New York, 1961, p. 321.

16 See: Kurt Mandelbaum's excellent 'Sozialdemokratie und Imperialismus' in *Sozialdemokratie und Leninismus: Zwei Aufsätze*, Berlin, 1974.

11. War pp. 90–95

1 S. E. Bronner (ed.), *The Letters of Rosa Luxemburg*, Boulder, Colorado, 1979, p. 157.
2 R. Luxemburg, 'The Junius pamphlet: the crisis in German social democracy' in M. Waters (ed.), *Rosa Luxemburg Speaks*, New York, 1970, p. 261.
3 *ibid.* pp. 316, 318.
4 *ibid.* p. 318.
5 *ibid.* p. 300.
6 *ibid.* p. 295.
7 *ibid.* pp. 302ff.
8 *ibid.* pp. 305–6.
9 *ibid.* p. 324.
10 *ibid.* p. 330.
11 See: H. Pachter, 'Was Weimar necessary' in *Dissent* (Winter, 1977) for an excellent analysis of the councils in relation to the needs of a republic.
12 See: A. Rosenberg, *History of the German Republic*, New York, 1965.
13 See: R. Luxemburg, 'Speech to the founding convention of the German Communist Party' in *Rosa Luxemburg Speaks*.
14 R. Luxemburg, 'Order reigns in Berlin' in R. Howard (ed.), *Selected Political Writings of Rosa Luxemburg*, New York, 1971, p. 415.

12. Rosa Luxemburg and Western Marxism pp. 96–104

1 P. Anderson, *Considerations on Western Marxism*, London 1976, p. 42.
2 See the introduction by Oskar Negt to N. Bucharin/A. Deborin, *Kontroversen über Dialektischen und Mechanistischen Materialismus* (Controversies over Dialectical and Mechanistic Materialism), Frankfurt, 1969.
3 Anderson, *Considerations on Western Marxism*, p. 56.
4 A clear example of such 'reflection theory' is Lenin's *Materialism and Empirio-Criticism*; for a superb criticism of reflection theory, see Korsch's *Marxism and Philosophy* as well as his essay

'15 thesen über wissenschaftlichen sozialismus' in E. Gerlach and J. Seifert (eds.), *Politische Texte*, Frankfurt, 1974.

5 See: R. Luxemburg, 'The stagnation of marxism' in M. Waters (ed.), *Rosa Luxemburg Speaks*, New York, 1970.

6 Luxemburg, 'Speech to the Hanover Congress (1899)', in *Rosa Luxemburg Speaks*, p. 47.

7 Luxemburg, Foreword to the anthology, *The Polish Question and the Socialist Movement* in H. B. Davis (ed.), *The National Question: Selected Writings by Rosa Luxemburg*, New York, 1976.

8 K. Korsch, *Marxism and Philosophy*, trans. F. Halliday, London, 1970, p. 92.

9 F. J. Raddatz, *Lukacs*, Hamburg, 1972, p. 60.

10 For Lukacs, the 'totality' is the 'methodological point of departure' for marxism. He recognizes Luxemburg's use of the concept and notes how it distinguishes her work from the works of her contemporaries in the Second International. G. Lukacs, *History and Class Consciousness: Studies in Marxist Dialectics*, trans. R. Livingstone, London, 1971, p. 9.

11 'Revisionism', of course, first emerges with Bernstein. But, though he proclaimed the 'critical' nature of his theory, he underplayed the role of class consciousness and undercut any notion of a mediated social 'totality'. Bernstein, therefore, remains on the same plane as his more orthodox opponents: See: Lukacs, 'Bernstein's triumph: notes on the essays written in honor of Karl Kautsky's seventieth birthday' in R. Livingstone (ed.), *Political Writings 1919–29*, London, 1972.

13 Rosa Luxemburg for the Present pp. 105–111

1 V. I. Lenin, 'Notes of a publicist' in M. Waters (ed.), *Rosa Luxemburg Speaks*, New York, 1970, p. 440.

2 S. E. Bronner (ed.), *The Letters of Rosa Luxemburg*, Boulder, Colorado, 1979, p. 147.

3 R. Luxemburg, 'The Russian revolution', in *Rosa Luxemburg Speaks*, pp. 389–90.

Index

129